The Balance Within: Nine Steps to a Purposeful Life

Shivang Patil

Published by Shivang Patil.

THE BALANCE WITHIN: NINE STEPS TO A PURPOSEFUL LIFE

Written by Shivang Patil.

Table of Contents

INTRODUCTION

Life often runs like a small dance between aspirations, relationships, and wellness. For most of us, finding harmony within ourselves and our surroundings feels almost impossible in today's fast world. However, true balance is not about flawlessness; it's about nurturing all aspects of our lives mentally, bodily, and spiritually and living through all those imperfections and vulnerabilities.

Inviting readers to engage with a transformative book on finding one's authentic self, healing wounds from the past, and creating a meaningful life based on purpose, resilience, and connection, ***The Balance Within: Nine Steps to a Purposeful Life*** represents a holistic answer for aligning values, actions, and emotions.

This is not only a book but also a companion for your journey. It's a reflective space where self-discovery meets growth. Each step inspires clarity, ignites action, and cultivates peace as we continue on the journey with courage and grace. Here we go!

Chapter 1: Discovering Your Authentic Self

Introduction:

Who are you, truly? Beneath the layers of societal expectations, familial roles, and self-imposed narratives lies the core of your being your authentic self. Discovering this essence is like peeling back the petals of a flower, one by one, to reveal its heart. This journey is not about reinventing yourself; it's about uncovering who you've always been.

Authenticity isn't a destination, it's a practice. It takes vulnerability, self-reflection, and strength. But as you get underway on this journey, you will realize that knowing and being your true self is the greatest freedom and satisfaction human existence can bestow upon anyone. May this chapter be your guide to embracing the unfiltered, unapologetic version of you.

1.1) Self-Discovery: The Blueprint to Living a Full Life

Introduction: Discovering the Real You

Imagine going on a journey of deep introspection in which every piece of you is viewed through a magnifying glass of awareness. What if, deep within your understanding of who you are, lies the key to living your purpose? Self-discovery is not just a concept; it is a transformation that forms the very fabric of your being. Every realization, every insight, is constructed block by block to build the reality you want to inhabit.

Quotes: Words that Enlighten

- *"Knowing yourself is the beginning of all wisdom."* — *Aristotle*
- *"The greatest discovery of my generation is that a human being can alter his life by altering his attitudes."* — *William James*
- *"Life isn't about finding yourself. Life is about creating yourself."* — *George Bernard Shaw*

Quotes remind us that this journey of self-discovery is empowering. The way we view ourselves directly correlates with the way we navigate our lives, guiding us toward an intentional and fulfilling existence.

Poem: The Dance of Self

"In silence's depths, where secrets dwell,

Stir the spirit up; its whispering tells.

A journey in, to the heart's gentle core,

Discovering treasures unseen and more.

There is nothing more liberating than seeing

The canvas of life unfurl itself through

Reflections of the past and dreams yet to be,

Shaped by every stroke of courage and every fight;

You define and illuminate existence."

This poem weaves together that complicated dance of self-discovery, showing precisely how our inner journey leads the way to purpose. Every thought creates ripples, echoing out through the very fabric of our experience.

Stories to Resonate With: Clara's Awakening

Imagine Clara: She was one of those lost souls swimming in the whirlwind of life. She was often indecisive, and fear, as well as opinions from others, clouded her thinking. One day, during a quiet moment of reflection, she asked herself this pivotal question: "Who am I when the expectations of society are stripped away?" Newfound courage arose in that moment; she embarked on a journey of self-discovery by recording her thoughts, finding passions, and discovering her voice. Within that introspective journey, Clara gained clarity and direction in her career as well as in her personal relationships.

From then on, she discovered her authentic self, which brought a purposeful life full of joy.

Exercises & Reflective Questions: Nurture Your Inner Life

Exercise: The Self-Discovery Journal

Save 30 minutes every day to write in a journal. Reflect on questions like "What are your core values?" or "What do you really enjoy?" Write without judgment, letting your thoughts flow wherever they want. At the end of each week, take time to read everything you have written for patterns or epiphanies.

Reflective Question:

As you think about your purpose in life, what do you feel? Are you excited, afraid, or uncertain? How do you see changing any negative thinking into positive, liberating thoughts?

Healing Moment

Sit comfortably, close your eyes, and take a deep breath. Recall a moment when you were totally present in your authentic life. What did you learn in that moment? Let yourself surrender to the sensations of that memory, holding onto the wisdom it imparts to your journey of self-discovery.

Cinematic Approach: Your Life as a Movie

Imagine yourself as the protagonist of a movie, with self-discovery being the story told. Chances are, in the beginning scene, you would be lost in the maze of societal expectations and doubts about who you really are. Suddenly, this film takes an interesting turn as you meet your ally such as a mentor, a book, or a transformative experience that invites you to explore in-depth who you are. As the story unfolds, you witness instances of victory; your newfound sense of self only fuels your actions and choices.

In the end, you realize that living with a reason is not about gaining, but about being your true self.

Conversations of Change: A Podcast Dialogue

Tune in to the exploratory session with Alex as he walks us through his journey of self-discovery and self-realization.

Alex: "Today, I want to share with you my journey of self-discovery. Isn't it cool how knowing oneself opens one's eyes to purpose? Most people try to find their fulfillment through outside validation, forgetting that they need to look inside themselves for fulfillment."

"I know someone named Jonah, who grappled deeply with his identity. After much introspection, he decided to ask himself, 'What do I really want?' That was it for him. He began to honor his passions and pursue his dreams unapologetically.

Self-discovery is a profound gift. What we find and know about ourselves is revolutionary. And so, I encourage you: Are you ready for your own journey? Each moment of introspection can unveil the layers of your identity waiting to be explored."

The Mindset Power: A Message of Motivation

It is the true you that catalyzes transformation. The clearer you are about who you are, the more consistent your choices will be with what you truly want. Imagine looking out at the world from your real self, where every challenge becomes an opportunity for growth and every setback a stepping stone to the purpose that you serve.

Remember, getting to know yourself does not happen overnight; rather, it unfolds piece by piece, petal by petal, much like the sun warming the flower as layers peel away to reveal your truest self.

Therapeutic Approach & Healing Moment: A Directed Change

Breathe. Close your eyes and think of something from the recent past that scared or upset you. What thoughts were associated with that moment? Were they born from fear, or are they your inner truth? Gently let those limiting beliefs go as you imagine a storyline in which you allow yourself to be yourself. Let this change inspire more peace and empowerment, bringing forth your true potential.

Lasting Insights: Being Your Authentic Self

You will discover in this important journey of self-discovery just how necessary it is for living a purposeful and fulfilling life. Every insight you gain brings you one step closer to the life you set out to live. Through getting to know yourself better, you gain the power to create your own reality.

Reflection Prompt/Closing Thoughts:

As you wander on this journey of exploration, make some time for reflection at this moment:

- How well do you know your true self?
- What can you do today that would be in line with what truly gives you purpose?
- What does it feel like for you to live every day as your most authentic self?

This journey truly begins from within; awareness fostered is the road to a life full of meaning and fulfillment.

1.2) Reflective Exercises and Uncovering Core Values

Introduction: Uncovering the Bedrock

Imagine yourself standing at the very edge of discovery, gazing into yourself to discover the true values that make you who you are. What if spending a few moments pondering your core values were the key to finding yourself in a more authentic life? Every value provides direction and significance to our experiences, like a beacon. They shape the choices we make, the bonds we foster, and even how we view obstacles. Learning about them is not only freeing; it is revolutionary.

Quotes: The Smarts of Wisdom

- *"Your values create your thoughts; your thoughts create your actions; your actions create your destiny."* — *Mahatma Gandhi*
- *"The privilege of a lifetime is to become who you truly are."* — *Carl Jung*

These quotes encapsulate the deep truth that what we value shapes our world. Being aware of and living by our values gives us the strength to live a life in harmony with what is important to us, thus amplifying our experience on all levels.

Poem: The Structure of Values

"In the stillness of the heart, values bloom,

Moistened by dreams, dark clouds consume.

A compass points to steer, a guiding hand

Reflecting the truth of one's sacred space.

Values form the trail we walk;

In their arms, we find our place.

What we love, we shall be,

The living breath, tapestry."

This poem speaks to the importance of knowing what is close to one's heart. It touches on how values shape our choices and participate in making a life full of meaning and happiness.

Anecdotal Accounts: The Discovery Experience

There was Tom, one of the best entrepreneurs out there; the challenges he faced were thoroughly bested by his skills, but he felt a chill inside, as if there was an emptiness within him. He would frequently ask, "What truly matters to me?" After joining a retreat targeted at self-reflection, a motivation for exploring his values came into place.

The first things that came to his mind were success, wealth, and recognition, but that was not the answer. He then explored deeper, through guided exercises, discovering values like integrity, community, and creativity. As soon as he started living his business in accordance with these values, not only did he feel a sense of fulfillment, but the quality of his life was revealed in ways he never dreamt of. Tom's transformation epitomizes the major shift that may occur when actions directly flow from core values.

Exercises & Reflective Questions: The Way to Clarity

Exercise:

The Values Inventory Spend a few minutes writing down 10 values that feel important to you. Then, reduce this list to your top 5 values. Think about why these values matter and how they guide your life on a day-to-day basis.

Reflective Question:

What values guide you in making decisions? Are they guiding you toward your highest self, or are they leading you astray?

Healing Moment:

Close your eyes and take a deep breath. Think of a moment in which you felt misaligned or lacked joy. What values were being compromised at that moment? Now think of this moment but honor your core values this time. What would the difference in experience be for you?

Cinematic Approach: Your Life as a Story

Imagine yourself in a movie. You are the hero, and your journey for authenticity begins. The movie opens with a wandering shot showing you crossing a hectic landscape of other people's expectations and phony values. Then, you run into a mentor, an old friend, or a good book. Such a defining moment an interior conversation that starts within reveals the worth of knowing your core values, which will make change possible. Therefore, only after walking through numerous trials will you find a shift in choices and experience a dramatic turnaround. The finale produces a character surrounded by his true self, enveloped by the richness of a fulfilling and joyful life.

Conversations of Change: A Podcast Dialogue

Values Unveiled: A Discussion with Maya and Jordan

Let's listen to a conversation between Maya and Jordan about understanding and embodying core values in life.

Maya: "Jordan, the discovery journey for our core values feels so intimidating yet empowering all at once. How did you start that journey for yourself?"

Jordan: "It began with a realization that the values I thought I held were often borrowed from others, and I felt disconnected. It was through a value exercise that I discovered what really resonated with my soul."

Maya: "Sounds enlightening. What did you find?"

Jordan: "For me, honesty and compassion were paramount. I realized that every action needs to reflect those values. As I move into them, I feel such a deep sense of peace and alignment."

Maya: "That says so much, Jordan. What advice do you have for someone stepping onto this path?"

Jordan:"Begin with authenticity. Ask yourself, 'What brings me joy?' The journey isn't always easy, but prioritizing self-reflection leads to clearer insights and a more fulfilling life."

And Maya reminds the listeners to embark on their own journey of discovering values and learning to tap into the wisdom within.

Power of Values: A Motivational Message

Living your values makes a difference. When the actions you take mirror what you truly care about, life is a journey of possibilities that is empowered. Never forget that values are dynamic and will shift as the individual does. Developing these guiding principles helps give us direction and satisfaction within ourselves.

Therapeutic Approach & Healing Moment: Guided Shift

Therapeutic Moment:

Take a deep breath in. Close your eyes. Remember when you felt that conflict with your values. What thoughts emerged in that moment? Acknowledge the sensations of confusion and frustration. Now, gently release those feelings and imagine a time when you acted in a way that honored your values. Let this empowering story imbue you with warmth and clarity. Knowing that to honor your true values is to enrich your emotional landscape and determine your reality.

Final Thought: Strength in Your Core

Your reality is a tapestry woven with the thread of your values, understood and lived by. Every single value becomes a rope that defines and stitches your identity and experience. When you identify and affix those core components, remember that they guide you toward a life of substance and authenticity.

Reflection Prompt/Closing Thoughts:

Reflect as you continue down this path of self-discovery:

- How clear are you on what you value most in life?
- What might alignment of your choices with your values look like in your everyday life?
- What would it feel like to live out every day more fully embracing your core values?

Your core values are who you are; they are what you base your life upon. Cultivating them opens the way to a more authentic and fulfilling life.

1.3) Vulnerability as Gateway to Authenticity

Introduction: The Beauty of Being Unfiltered

Imagine a world where you can let go of all pretenses and expose the real you without fear. What would it be if vulnerability were the gateway to your richest experiences? Every time you practice authenticity, you foster stronger connections with others and discover more about yourself. And yet, it is only when we let our true face show to the world that we discover our deepest power and the raw beauty of human relationships.

Quotes: Bringing to Light

- *"Vulnerability is not weakness; it's our greatest measure of courage. We ache to be seen, to be heard, to be understood. That vulnerability is where intimacy comes from." —* *Brené Brown*
- *"Your biggest self is on the other side of your biggest fear." — Maxwell Maltz"*
- *"Daring to set boundaries is about loving ourselves enough to allow logically appropriate boundaries with someone else." — Brené Brown*

These words are bright, lighting up the truth: vulnerability is not what keeps us away, but rather a bridge to an even more authentic existence. Through acceptance, we invite deeper connections and experiences into our lives.

Poem: The Strength in Vulnerability

"In shadows still, where fears reside,

Lean in close; let love abide.

The cracks that mar, they softly gleam.

In vulnerability, we find our dream.

Each scar a story, each tear a tale,

Embracing truth, we shall not fail.

In open hearts, the world finds grace;

Authenticity, our rightful place."

This poem touches on the paradox of vulnerability: it is in the cracks that the light gets in, creating a narrative of authenticity that can lead to connection with self and others.

Relatable Stories: The Transformational Journey

Sam was an exceptional artist who suffered from the shackles of judgmental fear. He had always showcased only the well-crafted pieces, fearing that the rough drafts would be criticized. One evening, his friend suggested that Sam reveal all the struggles behind his art, showcasing the imperfect journey of creation.

Deep-breathing into the act, Sam nervously chose to share his precious drafts, failures, and unformed emotions braided together with every stroke. To his surprise, the response was overwhelmingly positive. People warmed to honesty; the messiness of creation was beautiful. This insight revealed a crucial truth to Sam: when he made himself vulnerable, he could open himself up to greater connections, authenticity, and richness in his artistic expression.

Exercises & Reflective Questions: Authenticity

Exercise: Vulnerability Diary

Write for a week in a diary. Each day, reflect on a moment when you felt vulnerable. What emotions did you experience, and how did it affect your day? At the end of the, review what you've written. What can you learn from your vulnerability to openness?

Reflective Question:

When was the last time you were vulnerable? What did you learn about yourself in that moment? Does that vulnerability deepen your connections with others?

Healing Moment:

Take a moment to close your eyes and breathe deeply. Remember that moment when you shared a part of yourself that scared you or felt raw. What was the shift in mood or relationship with others? What did it feel like to let go and be seen? Imagine letting go of fears tied to vulnerability.

Cinematic Technique: Your Real Self on Display

Now, imagine yourself in the scene of a movie. You are standing before an audience for a presentation. In the opening scenes, you feel the heavy pressure of the demand, and you struggle with the desire to comply. Then comes the turning point: a smiling face in the audience, a nod, or a warm smile that consoles you.

The camera captures your transformation as you begin to speak authentically; the real you shines through without apology. Every word feels lighter, and the crowd responds with empathy, laughter, and connection. In the final scene, authenticity breeds unity; you've created a shared experience, breaking down barriers and embracing the beautiful mess that you are.

Conversations of Change: A Podcast Dialogue

The Vulnerability Hour: Roundtable Discussion on Authenticity

Join us as we engage in a lively roundtable discussion with Mia, Liam, Sabrina, and David, speaking about the profundity of embracing vulnerability.

Mia: "Today, we unpack vulnerability and how it serves as a pathway to authenticity. Liam, what does vulnerability mean to you?

Liam: "To me, vulnerability is power. It's unveiling the real me despite all the risks that come with it. Whenever I share my fears, I sometimes find strength in honesty.

Sabrina: "Absolutely! It is like peeling layers. Every layer brings out more of who we are beneath societal expectations. When we show our scars, we can connect and grow with others.

David: "I agree, Sabrina. I used to run away from vulnerability, but once I allowed people to be really real with me, I unlocked the true power of support and understanding around me.

Liam: "Start small. Share a personal story with someone you trust and observe how it feels to expose that part of you.

Sabrina: "I would say practice self-compassion. You don't have to be perfect to deserve love and affection.

David: "Second, remember that vulnerability is not weakness but strength. It opens channels for real connections.

Mia: "Let's remind everyone that vulnerability is a significant step toward authenticity. It's not about viewing you; it's about embracing you for who you truly are."

The Power of Authenticity: A Motivational Message

Transformation through vulnerability does not depend on what is coming from others; it depends on you. When you accept yourself for who you are, you open up space for greater truths to reveal themselves, deeper connections to form, and the courage to live life in a way that comes most naturally to you.

Therapeutic Approach & Healing Moment: A Guided Shift

Therapeutic Moment:

Take a deep breath. For a moment, reflect on a time when vulnerability became too much to bear. Allow yourself to feel it without judgment. Now imagine framing that same event as a growth opportunity rather than an occasion for rejection. Instead of saying, "I am going to get rejected," you might say, "Perhaps I am loved for who I am." Let yourself move into that space of empowerment and acceptance, where vulnerability is connection and healing.

Final Thought: Inner Truth

Your strength to be honest with yourself resides inside of you. Every moment you honor your vulnerability brings you one step closer to living the life you want a life filled with substantive relationships and authentic expressions. Through this courage, you build your power to connect and manifest a reality that reflects who you are.

Reflection Prompt/Closing Thoughts:

Consider these questions as you continue on this path:

- How comfortable are you with your vulnerabilities?
- What is one small act of vulnerability you can commit to today to create authenticity?
- What would your life be like if you felt the courage to be perfectly true to yourself in all moments?

Your authentic self is waiting. Soften through acceptance and love, creating a canvas for a life vibrating with your deepest and most meaningful connections.

Chapter 2: Building Resilience Through Healing

Introduction:

Life has those moments where it feels like everything is crashing around us. It's at these moments that challenges, loss, and pain seem to just surround us. Imagine you're in the middle of that kind of storm. Well, what if I were to tell you that within such storms are very strong elements waiting to be drawn out? That's the beauty of resilience. It is not merely survival, but triumph over adversity. Resilience is the strength to come up from the ashes, to find new meaning in struggle, and to emerge stronger than ever. It is the inner force guiding us toward healing and personal growth, reminding us that though life may break us, it cannot defeat us.

As you read this chapter, you will learn how resilience is cultivated and how it enables us not only to endure but to transform our experiences into opportunities for healing. By the end of this chapter, you will see resilience not as a static trait but as an evolving skill, nurtured through introspection, compassion, and action.

2.1) What Is Resilience, and How Does It Safeguard Us from Trouble?

Introduction: Strength

Imagine standing at the edge of a storm, the rain pouring down and the wind howling life throwing everything it has at you. What if I told you that within this turmoil lies the essence of resilience? It's more than just bouncing back; it is an unwavering strength that allows us to navigate through life's challenges. Resilience is the inner buoyancy that prevents us from sinking under adversity. It invites new perspectives and helps us see the hurdles that come as opportunities for growth. Resilience can also help us light our way through the darkest paths and guide us toward a brighter horizon.

Quotes: Wisdom That Resonates

- *"Resilience is not about never falling, but about rising every time we fall."—Nelson Mandela*
- *"Life doesn't get easier or more forgiving; we get stronger and more resilient."—Steve Maraboli*
- *"The oak fought the wind and lived, while the willow bent to ease."—Robert Jordan*

These words convey a profound truth: our strength is found in how we recover, renew, and rise again. They remind us that resilience is not a gift but a learned competence over time.

Poem: The Dance with Adversity

"In the storm, we discover ourselves.

When life breaks us, we learn to be free.

Resilience dances on broken ground.

In every struggle, there is a found strength.

Like rivers running through stones that are mighty and strong,

We bend but do not break and move along.

For in each one, we rise anew;

A test of spirit, resilient and true."

This poem typifies the journey of resilience, showing that in adversity, we find inner strength. It also speaks to the subtleties of resilience and how trials ignite a transformation within us.

Stories to Relate: Triumph Through Trials

Consider Marcus, a musical genius whose talents are set to unfold on a stage. That was a fateful night when his hand was shattered in an accident that silenced him from years of heart wrenching music. All of a sudden, he found himself facing despair and frustration at a crossroads. However, during those dark times, a shred of resilience arose when he embraced his pain, redefined his passion, and turned toward music production. Instead of defeat, he learned a new way of being with the melodies he loved. He transformed his misery into a symphony, proving that resilience allows us to turn wounds into wisdom.

Exercises & Reflective Questions: Building Your Resilience Muscle

Exercise: Resilience Reflection Journal

For one week, write in a journal to note the times when adversity arises. Record your first reactions and the decisions you make afterward. Reflect on what decisions either undermine or support your ability to bounce back. By the end of the week, you should see any patterns that emerge.

Reflective Question:

Is it hope that leads you into challenges, or a fight against fear? Does this attitude help you develop better elasticity to find resilience?

Healing Moment:

Take a few moments to breathe deeply in a quiet space. Choose a difficulty you have faced lately. What thoughts come up for you? Which moments of resilience have you lived through? Imagine that obstacle dissipating, holding on to the power of being able to rise.

Film Thematic Strategy: The Resilience Story

Imagine your life as a movie, each episode a victory of strength. The opening scene of the movie shows how the challenges of life appear to be insurmountable mountains. But as the movie progresses, moments of strong support from friends, mentors, or deep insights come into the picture. Then, you heroically navigate the straits of challenge, and the apparent weaknesses in the plot turn out to be developmental. Climax: How this strength not only makes one person a better citizen but also influences all whom someone touches. The final shot the credits roll leaves a powerful legacy of strength and hope for others to follow.

Conversations of Change: A Podcast Dialogue

Reflections on Resilience: Ava's Insightful Journey.

Let's hear from Ava about the power of change through resilience.

Ava: "Today I want to share with you the power of resilience. It is easy to be conquered by life when it brings us down. But what if I told you that each time we fall, it is actually a rallying cry? I want to tell you a story about my friend Ray. He just lost his job quite unexpectedly. Completely devastated by what seemed like a downturn in his life, he chose to see this setback as the moment to turn his life around. He started working every day toward a new passion: he began expressing his art. With time, this fall was not the end but a beginning.

"It is the truth. Resilience feeds on the belief that we are capable of transforming our reality from the pit of despair. Challenge me to ask you this: What do you want to grow from your struggles? And resilience is our light."

Ava ends with a call to action for all listeners, encouraging them to discover their inner strength as they navigate through difficulty. Every small act of courage forms the ultimate narrative of resilience.

The Strength of Resilience: A Message of Motivation

The heart of resilience does not lie in endurance alone. It is the art of thriving as one endures. The perspective through which you view challenges changes your experience. As you build resilience, opportunities start to unfurl among the burdens. Every setback holds within it the seed of potential; it inspires you to dig deeper, grow stronger, and emerge more profound.

Therapeutic Approach & Healing Moment: A Facilitated Change of Direction

Therapeutic Moment:

Now close your eyes. Take several deep breaths and think about a situation in which you faced a significant challenge. Reflect: What were your feelings while experiencing this? What thoughts kept recurring in your mind? Were they filled with despair or hope? Gently let go of all negative thoughts. Visualize the story of yourself becoming resilient and powerful. Change your mindset from "I can't" to "What if I could?". Believe in this vision and let it inspire you with strength.

Thought to Live for Today: Your Resilient Spirit

There is nothing easy about the path to resilience; it is a journey into yourself, with every thought and every experience serving as a brushstroke on your canvas. As you cultivate resilient thinking, you will inspire that in others as well. Life's frustrations are not merely speed bumps but actually stepping stones to beginnings based on what we have learned about ourselves.

Reflection Prompt/Closing Thoughts:

As you follow your path, make time to reflect on:

- How attuned are you to your responses to adversity?
- What slight shift in perspective could amplify your resilience?
- What would life with an unyielding faith in your ability to triumph feel like?

Accept your journey. Resilience is the key that unlocks the best in you.

2.2) Ways to Work Through Past Pain and Trauma

Introduction: The Road Within

Think for a moment about the emotional landscapes of your life. Carry in your mind the weight of past pain and trauma, like a knapsack, with each new experience adding a stone to define your road. What if you could begin to lighten this load? What if you understood that you need to unpack these experiences and learn from them rather than leaving them inside? The reminiscence of the pangs, each shroud of trauma, teaches a lesson a step forward in your life journey toward growth and transformation.

Quotes: Wisdom That Leads

- *"The wound is the place where the Light enters you." — Rumi"*
- *"Pain is inevitable, but suffering is optional." — Haruki Murakami*
- *"The greatest healing therapy is friendship and love." — Hubert H. Humphrey*

These profound words remind us that pain is something everyone faces, but how we choose to grapple with it is what will shape our healing narrative. Each quote acts like a lighthouse beacon, guiding us to understand that our response to past trauma unlocks the potential for profound personal growth.

Poem: The Resilience of the Heart

"Through the shadows of fate's hard hand,

The heart learns things we can't understand.

Through tears that wash the dust away,

We rise anew on each new day.

Breathe in the struggle; breathe out the pain.

From cracks in our hearts, love will remain."

This poem encapsulates the strength of resilience that exists in every human experience. It resonates with the empowering strength of accepting pain, from which we emerge even stronger and wiser from our battles.

Stories of Common Life: Strides Toward Wholeness

Consider the story of Marcus, who was tormented by traumatic experiences during childhood. For years, he resisted those ugly wounds of neglect and abandonment. The result? He spent an unhappy childhood in relationships throughout his adulthood and felt he was never good enough. After several years of inner conflict, a therapist asked him, "What if your past doesn't define your future?" That simple and powerful question led Marcus on a journey to discover himself.

He attended support groups, listening to how other people narrated their experiences. Gradually, he opened up about what had actually been happening to him, coming to realize that he wasn't the only one. With every story unfolding like a puzzle, parts of him were gradually revealed in fragments: first, he would confront his past and recognize his pain; then transform those burdens into insight, setting the stage for a future filled with connection and hope.

Exercises & Reflective Questions: Healing Exercise

Exercise: The Healing Letter

Write a letter to your past self. Open yourself up: validate the pain, acknowledge the struggle, and express compassion. Let this letter be a bridge between your past and your present. Consider sharing it with a trusted friend or therapist, or just keep it as a reminder of how far you have come.

Reflective Question:

What past experience is still lingering in your mind and keeping you from moving forward? How do you feel this experience would change your perspective of who you are and what you could become?

Healing Moment:

Close your eyes and imagine a safe space where you could meet your younger self. What words of comfort and nourishment would you offer to care for them? Hold onto this moment, nurturing understanding and healing within.

Cinematic Method: Your Life in a Movie

Envision yourself as the protagonist in the movie that makes up the tapestry of your emotions. The early scenes are flashbacks of pain moments that have attempted to define you. But with each new scene, you meet crucial characters: a mentor, a friend, and moments of revelation through books or conversations that inspire you to face your past. The camera records your bold entry into healing, the slow uncovering of colors as you finally find acceptance of your fragility. The closing credits serve as a powerful testament to your strength as you stand tall, shining light forged in adversity.

Dialogue of Change: A Podcast Conversation

Healing through Connection: A Dialogue between Jasmine and Ethan

Jasmine: "Ethan, in reflecting on my pain, I have found it beautiful to witness how some experiences can freeze you in your tracks or motivate you to take action for change. What about you?"

Ethan: "Absolutely, Jasmine. Until then, my traumatic past was running my current life. This simple question changed everything: 'What if I could see my pain as a teacher?'"

Jasmine: "That is so powerful. Where did this shift in perspective begin for you?"

Ethan: "I started journaling, putting down whatever was in my head and heart. It was a messy process, but with every word, I felt lighter. I realized that my story wasn't so much about survival but truly about transformation."

Jasmine: "Such a beautiful way to redefine the narrative. For those listening, what wisdom do you have for them?"

Ethan: "Lean into the pain, embracing it, acknowledging it without letting it define you. Every experience carries lessons that open your heart to discover them."

A Message of Hope

There is a deep truth resonating within us all: our healing capacity lives in our thoughts. Change the way we think about pain and trauma, and in that manner, change our relationship with such problems. Let us not permit them to function as anchors but rather as catalysts that will inspire our growth. Healing does not come from outside; it is born from within. It blows upon the spark of resilience and power.

Therapeutic Approach & Healing Moment: Guided Visualization

Therapeutic Moment:

Take a minute. Close your eyes and breathe deeply. Imagine a circumstance that hurt you quite badly. Now, imagine covering that wound with compassion. What would kindness feel like in that space? How would it feel to let go of the grip resentment has and choose forgiveness instead? Allow that warmth to fill you, knowing you are reclaiming your story.

Final Thought: Acceptance of Your Story

You get to choose to change your story. Own the pain, delve into its depths, but understand that your story doesn't end there. With each bold step toward recovery, with each thought and each emotion that is acknowledged, healing begins. The past has molded you, but it needn't hold you captive. Let it instead be the rich soil from which your most radiant self can bloom.

Reflection Prompt/Closing Thoughts:

As you move forward on this healing path, take some time for reflection:

- What has led to where you are today?
- How would you tell a new story of your life in a way that empowers your healing?
- What would it be like for you to be held by kindness and compassion, understanding your past but not being defined by it as you move forward?

Let go of the power of your story; it is the only key to your emancipation and integration. Loving the healing within your heart is the foundation for building a vibrant and empowered future.

2.3) Significance of Self-Compassion in the Healing Journey

Introduction: Loveliness Grows From Within

Stand in front of the mirror, not just to look at your image, but to really see yourself: your imperfections, your suffering, your fight. What would happen if, instead of judgment or criticism, you bestowed upon yourself the same tender loving care that you'd give to a friend in pain? In the healing journey, that balm which soothes the soul and heals the heart is self-compassion. It's about knowing our common humanity and being deserving of love and acceptance, even at our worst.

Quotes: Seeds of Enlightenment

- *"Talk to yourself like someone you love."* — Brené Brown
- *"Self-compassion is simply giving the same kindness to ourselves that we would give to others."* — Christopher Germer
- *"The strongest relationship you'll ever have is the relationship with yourself."* — Steve Maraboli

These quotes whisper a deep truth: self-compassion is not a soft and indulgent practice but an integral part of healing. They remind us that how we treat ourselves fundamentally influences the path we tread.

Poem: The Gentle Whisper of Self-Love

"The quiet moments: feel the grace,

When tender words embrace your space.

Forgive your flaws, let go of shame,

For healing starts when you claim your name.

Wearing kindness in a warm embrace,

The heart will learn its proper place.

Every scar is a tale, every tear a sign,

In self-compassion, you will shine."

This poem captures the nurturing aspect of self-compassion. It uses the language of tender acceptance of human imperfection and the redeeming potency of love.

Stories to Identify With: The Story of Redemption

Let's share Sarah's story of a woman who fought against the heavy weight of self-criticism. With years of relentless perfectionism, she spiraled down, unable to glimpse any beautiful aspects of her journey. A chance encounter with a self-compassion workshop led her to reassess the episodes of her life. "What if I treated myself with the same kindness that I offered others?" she wondered.

As she learned not to judge her suffering, something great was happening. Gentle affirmations such as "I am enough" and "I deserve love" replaced the critical voice. Her reality began to shift slowly, pressure and stress started to lower, joy flooded back into her life, and her heart opened up to all that love had always sought. The story of Sarah shows that living self-compassion can be a real trigger for deep change.

Exercises & Reflective Questions: Cultivating Inner Warmth

Exercise: The Self-Compassion letter

Take a minute to write yourself a letter during a difficult time. Share all your feelings with yourself, without judgment, trying to understand your thoughts and speak kindly to yourself. Read it aloud and let the words settle deep inside you.

Reflective Question:

How do you generally react when you mess up? Are those thoughts helpful?

Healing Moment:

Close your eyes and breathe several times. Imagine the time when you were cruel to yourself. Now imagine surrounding that moment with kindness. What does it feel like to be this tender with yourself? Let this feeling soak into you, carrying with it a sense of calm.

Cinematic Approach: Your Life as a Redemption Movie

Imagine your life as if it's a film beautifully shot. It begins with the opening scene where you are drowned in self-doubt and self-blame. However, the plot twist comes when the power of self-compassion arrives in the form of words from a wise mentor or a transformative book. Thus, while sailing through your opposition, you learn to love yourself tenderly as you rewrite the narrative from shame to acceptance. In the last frame, standing tall and shining bright with your authenticity, thank yourself for all that you have learned.

Discussions of Change: Podcast Conversation

The Compassionate Heart: A Discussion about Self-Love.

Let's step into a conversation with Sarah, James, Mia, and Ethan on how self-compassion makes all things new.

Sarah: "Today, we're going to tackle something significant in the healing process but actually, something much more critical to most people: self-compassion. James, why do you think it is so important?"

James: "Self-compassion is that safe haven where growth is nurtured. Being vulnerable allows us to heal deep down."

Mia: "Absolutely! It is a warm hug for our inner child. We need that comfort to prosper."

Ethan: "I've found that the more you practice self-compassion, the more resilient you become toward life. It is a gift you can give yourself."

Sarah: "If listeners feel they are struggling with self-criticism, what would you say to them?"

James: "Start with tiny good deeds toward yourself. Enjoy each step forward, no matter how ridiculously minor it seems."

Mia: "Introduce daily affirmations. Tell yourself every day that you deserve to be loved."

Ethan: "And flaws are human. Grow from there."

Sarah: "These are great insights. Remember, the journey to self-compassion is not a destination but a practice worth cultivating."

The Power of Self-Compassion: A Message of Hope

Universal healing truth: self-compassion is the best cure for suffering. It opens up the soul and helps us accept ourselves wholly, allowing us to learn from the experiences of life without judgment. When individuals turn toward themselves with compassion, a world of possibilities for love to grow emerges, and growth will surely happen.

Therapeutic Approach & Healing Moment: A Guided Reflection

Therapeutic Moment:

Sit comfortably. Close your eyes and breathe. Recall a situation in the past in which you felt extreme pain or regret. Reflect on what you would say to that version of yourself. Were you hard on yourself? Now imagine a comforting but firm voice that can come forth to comfort and affirm you. Instead of saying, "I wish I hadn't," let the thought become, "I am learning and growing every day." Receive this nourishing energy, knowing it empowers you on your healing journey.

Afterword: Your Inner Refuge

Healing is a journey of self-compassion. Each gentle thought and reflection cultivates within you a refuge where love and acceptance abound. Through self-compassion, you regain your strength to heal and flourish.

Reflection Exercise/Closing Reading:

Reflect on the following as you enter this healing journey:

- What is the frequency with which you are kind to yourself daily?
- How do you turn self-criticism into self-compassion?
- What would your life look like if self-love were a practice you engaged in as naturally as breathing?

Your heart is a garden that blooms with tender care.
Tending it with self-compassion sets you on a path to
building a life full of love, healing, and all the possibilities.

Chapter 3: Transforming Fear into Fuel for Growth

Introduction:

Fear is often viewed as a thing to be overcome or feared, but what if fear were the fuel that launched one toward growth? Here in this chapter, we explore how fear can be a propellant for personal development, not a deterrent. Understanding the difference between healthy and debilitating fear, we can start reframing our mindset and harnessing the energy of fear to push us beyond our comfort zones. Whether it is confronting long-held anxieties or facing new challenges, this chapter will provide practical tools to help you transform fear from a limiting force into a source of strength and resilience.

3.1) Healthy vs. Debilitating Fear

Introduction: Understanding the Fear Factor

A primer on emotion fear is a human emotion, a primal force that may save us or paralyze us. Imagine facing the edge of a very cliff, your heart pounding, instincts screaming at you backward. This healthy fear is an alarm that keeps you safe. But then there is the fear that holds you back, preventing you from moving forward. This is crippling. We must learn to discern these two types of fear in order to arm ourselves and move forward through life.

Quotes: Words of the Wise

- *"Fear doesn't stop death; it stops life." — Victor Hugo*
- *"Do one thing every day that scares you." — Eleanor Roosevelt*
- *"Courage is not the absence of fear, but the triumph over it." — Nelson Mandela*

These strong words conjure up the very concept that, if used with the intention of change, fear is something that catalyzes development rather than something to keep one's distance from. Healthy fear moves toward a goal and achieves great leaps into the unknown. Debilitating fear stagnates, locks us within chains of the past, and clouds our view of the future.

Poem: The Bifaced Nature of Fear

"In twilight lurks a feeling deep,

Protecting, wise, yet often steep.

Healthy fear, a guiding light,

In the darkest night, illuminates paths.

Yet sometimes fear, a heavy chain,

Whispers lie and fosters pain.

Debilitating doubt, a tempest tossed,

Incites a battle where dreams are lost."

This poem sums up the duplicity of fear: healthy fear being a beacon, and debilitating fear being darkness that chains our capacity and acuteness.

The Relatable Stories: Alex's Fearful Trail

Imagine Alex: an emerging artist who wants to paint, with healthy fear present as he prepares for his maiden exhibition. This fear compels him to refine his pieces, practice his presentation, and engage with other artists. But soon, a paralyzing fear creeps in. "Not being liked by anyone will ruin my work" now sweeps through the excitement of his dream. He gets caught up in doubt; that paralyzing fright from the power of creativity knocks him back into the very platform he yearns to embrace.

With a mentor to guide him, Alex learns to acknowledge his fears but not to allow them to drive his decision-making. Through thought reformulation, he shifts from a mindset of limitation to one of empowerment. He realizes that fear is a natural part of the artistic process; soon enough, he can stand behind his pieces with confidence.

Exercises & Reflective Questions: Tempering Fear

Exercise: Fear Inventory

Make a list of fears that come to mind healthful and debilitating alike. Beside each, label it "triggers action" or "holds me back." Consider times when confronting your fear has led to growth.

Reflective Question:

What fears are currently informing your choices? Do they protect you or paralyze you?

Healing Moment:

Close your eyes and breathe. Recall a time when you faced a fear that felt insurmountable. How has that experience shaped your world today? What new opportunities opened up for you from that moment on? This image will be the strength that inspires you to recall those strengths.

The Cinematic Method: Your Fear as a Plot Line

Imagine your life as a movie in which an exciting plot unfolds. The hero or heroine reaches a decision point and moves along with healthy fear toward dear relationships and thrilling adventures. However, there is a debilitating fear that alternates throughout the plot to be fearful, to miss opportunities, to doubt which casts shadows over the steps of the hero.

Now it gets interesting as we introduce the film's critical character, a mentor or a profound moment of realization. The catalyst for change is not just an enemy; it's now an accompanying travel companion: fear. Ultimately, the movie ends with the protagonist finding their strength, but this is all wrapped in the knowledge that fear will always be there, but doesn't have to control one's script.

Dialogues of Change: A Reflective Conversation

Confronting Fear: A Conversation with Jenna

Jenna: "Today, I want to explore something that all of us face: the ongoing battles with fear. Sometimes my heart races, and it's that gentle push I need to rise; at other times, fear immobilizes me."

Jenna continues, "I remember one day when I thought it was scary to speak in front of people at a community event. My brain was racing with thoughts about my ability. A friend of mine said, 'What if you focus on the impact you could make rather than the fear?' That completely shifted everything for me."

"I learned to replace anxiety with purpose by embracing healthy fear as a driving force for connection and authenticity."

So today, consider every fear you experience. Ask yourself: Is it urging you forward or dragging you down into despair? The lens through which you view your fears can change the very experience of your fears themselves.

The Transformative Power of Fear

Fear is an incredibly complex emotion, but understanding its subtleties allows us to use it as a tool rather than something binding. When healthy fear prompts growth, we empower ourselves to accept new experiences, take bold challenges, and build resilience that helps us travel well. Debilitating fear, on the other hand, chains us in a life of limitation. By acknowledging the forms it takes, we regain our power and relive our stories.

Therapeutic Approach & Healing Moment: A Guided Reflection

Therapeutic Moment:

Take a breath in and look at a fear that haunts you. Is this fear protective or somehow constrictive? Imagine a soft, golden light surrounding this fear. See it growing with each breath, filling out all the truth and insight waiting there. What empowering belief could take residence in that space where the shadow of your fear currently resides? Make this a visualization for transformation that will allow you to move forward with renewed energy.

Final Thought: Your Relationship with Fear

Your relationship with your fears might have a huge impact on your journey. When tapped into as a motivator, positive fear stirs you. When debilitating, it tells you to stop, reflect, and change direction. By becoming aware of the conditions causing the fear and by reframing your thoughts, you might just convert the right fears into stepping stones toward purpose and fulfillment.

Reflection Prompt/Closing Thoughts:

As you walk through your relationship with fear, take a moment to reflect:

- How do you differentiate between healthy and debilitating fear in your life?
- What small actions can you take to shift debilitating fears into opportunities for growth?
- Imagine living each day with a mindset of courage and tenacity. How would that transform your reality?

Fear is the compass that will show you who you are when you mean to carry it in. Own it, because the road belongs to you.

3.2) Strategies for Finding and Reframing Triggers and Mindset Strategies

Introduction: Unpacking the Causes of Fear

Fear is a web intricately woven through thought processes, experience, and perception. What if you came to realize that fear, rather than being a force that paralyzes you, is, in fact, your signal a guide to areas in your life that you have to transform? Every anxious heartbeat means an opportunity to grow, and understanding the trigger factors is important for forming a new mindset. The journey begins with realizing that fear is not the enemy but a guide that takes us into inner territory.

Quotes: Brighten Your Visions

- *"The only thing we have to fear is fear itself." — Franklin D. Roosevelt*
- *"Fear is only as deep as the mind allows." — Japanese Proverb*

These musings remind us that, although we may be paralyzed by fear, it is a potent energy force upon which we can learn to make our way. Each quote serves as a different window through which we come to view our fears; they nudge us into facing them rather than fleeing from them.

Poem: The Heart of Transformation

"In dark fears,

Doubts we cannot conceal.

But courage stirs within the heart,

The strength to find our part.

Like dawn breaking over a darkened past,

A steadfast light in which we stand at last,

A shift of mind, a light that never fades.

With every little step, we grow to stand,

Transforming fear with a steady hand."

This poem indeed describes transformation, transformation from fear to empowerment. It highlights the grace of understanding that fears are only stepping stones and not stop signs, where one may change their approach.

Relatable Stories: Rediscovering Strength

Consider Jacob, the young, talented artist paralyzed by the fear of judgment. His inner critic loomed large over him, whispering quietly in his ear that what he was making wasn't good enough. A casual conversation with a friend led Jacob to ask himself, "What if your greatest

masterpiece comes out of what you're afraid to share?"
This singular question stirred something deep within him.

Out of his leap of faith, Jacob began to explore the very
pieces he feared to share. When he finally showed them,
the reception was overwhelmingly positive. His fright
turned into a newfound sense of belonging and validity in
life that reflects through the colors and creativity he kept
inside himself. What he once tolerated as something that
stifled his voice became the catalyst for connection.

Exercises & Reflective Questions: Accepting Awareness

Exercise: Fear Mapping

Take time to draw your fears. Find a quiet place and take
out a sheet of paper. Record each fear that you have,
creating branches of other thoughts and emotions that
come off it. This visual chart helps break down where
those fears come from and facilitates gaining more clarity
and understanding.

Reflective Question:

What is the first thing that you think of when fear starts
creeping into the picture? How does that then play out in
inaction or action?

Healing Moment:

Close your eyes and breathe in deeply. Reflect on a time
when fear held you back from doing something you

wanted to do. The hazy thoughts cloud your sight. Now, intentionally replace each fear ridden thought with a related, empowering affirming thought. What new directions do thought pathways open up when you do this?

Cinematic Approach: Your Path to Transformation

Picture walking into the cinema, where the hero is disrupted by crippling fears that dictate the storyline. But there is a turning point in the form of a guide, an illuminator in the darkness. The camera captures this journey of movement from what has been to the tapestry woven with courage and possibility. Each scene becomes more difficult; yet, still, the hero learns to be vulnerable, crafting a great story saturated with authenticity and power. The climax unfolds as they finally confront their greatest fear, empowered and redefined a living testament to the power of a mindset shift.

Conversations of Change: A Podcast Dialogue

Facing Fear: A Dialogue Between Zoe and Sam

Zoe: "Sam, with the way fears mold our behavior, it's absolutely fascinating how they can either bind or set free. Where would you say your journey started with facing fear?"

Sam: "It was this dawning realization that fear had become my default setting. I often retreated into my comfort zone, avoiding anything I feared was a challenging kind of living in black and white. But then a friend nudged me to explore this question: 'What if fear is just a doorway, not a wall?"

Zoe: "That's incredibly powerful. So in what ways did that begin to shift your approach?"

Sam: "It has been life changing for me. I started with something tiny every day that I would have otherwise avoided doing. While each success encouraged me to go further, confidence began to unfurl. It was as if parts of myself that had been asleep were being rediscovered. Fear became not a chain but a guide."

Zoe: "Such an empowering view! What advice would you give to anybody stuck in their fears?"

Sam: "Awareness is key. Begin with the knowledge that fear exists within you, but it does not have to be in the driver's seat of your choices. Defeat one fear at a time. Rejoice in those small victories, for they all add up to transformative power."

As her dialogue wanes, Zoe sums up what she has learned: accepting fear as a means to personal progress opens doors to a more meaningful, authentic life.

The Power of Mindset: A Motivational Message

Here lies the transformative power of your mindset: redefined fear that once in your way obstacle now becomes an essential ingredient in your recipe for success.

Ultimately, the way you tackle your fears will set the tone for your journey. By changing your connection with fear, you begin shifting where every second is a cause for celebration instead of something that blocks your path. Remember, you have within you a set of tools that can reshape your story into a tapestry of growth and resilience.

Therapeutic Approach & Healing Moment: A Guided Transition

Therapeutic Approach

Deep breathe in and let a nourishing breath go. Envision a time you felt hostage to fear. What were the thoughts serving that fear? Were they confining or attached to a false notion? Receive them, then slowly exhale each confining notion. Envision yourself stepping into that space of fear and placing it instead within curiosity. What is it about walking in the unknown that you can find and absorb in that place? Let that vision spread warmth and strength within you and prepare your soil for new beginnings.

Final Thought: Tapping into Your Inner Strength

You have the power to know and define what fear is. Every idea and belief build not only the perception of reality but also the lived experience. By consciously deciding to own those fears, you walk toward a reality that your true human potential creates. Never forget that fears are only signposts

on the road to growth, and your mind is the compass
guiding this journey through life.

Reflection Prompt/Closing Thoughts:

As you enter into this process of identifying fears and
reframing your mindset, consider the following:

- How often do you let fear guide your decisions?
- What is one tiny thing you can do today to start
  shifting this dynamic for yourself?
- Envision living in a space of curiosity rather than
  fear. How would that feel?

Thoughts are the keys unlocking a potential life that is
resourceful. By embracing your fears and cultivating your
growth oriented mindset, you create a backdrop for a
future full of possibilities.

3.3) Actual Practice to Overcome Feared Things Gradually

Introduction: Fear the evil we construct

Imagine this: you stand at the edge of a cliff, and the
ground appears all set to swallow you in. This, my friend, is
fear, a product of the mind that paralyzes us, keeping us
away from the lives we want. Think about this: what if the
very fears looming before you are only shadows conjured

by your thoughts? What if you could take apart these shadows piece by piece, unveiling truth after truth? It is often in the unknown that fear lurks an extension of what we believe and perceive. And when we open that door to gradual confrontation.

Quotes: Voices of Wisdom

- *"The brave man is not he who does not feel afraid, but he who conquers that fear."* — *Nelson Mandela*

These great words of wisdom light the path of fear. They remind us that everyone should have some degree of fear within them because it accompanies human nature, but it doesn't have to limit anyone.

Poem: Steps into the Dance with Fear

'Fear is a shadow, sometime afterthought,

A whispered word, a feeling we sought.

Step into darkness; light up with courage bright,

With every small step, reclaim your light.

Fear can be tamed; it's a spirit to guide,

With patience and practice, let faith stride.

For every small victory, you build a fortress.

Embrace the darkness; let your heart overflow."

This poem describes the delicate dance we make with our fears. It underscores the notion that fear can be a catalyst and turn into an anchor that leads us toward growth and self-discovery.

Relatable Stories: The Journey of Confrontation

Let's just imagine this: Liam is an artist. He is good, but he fears having his works put on public display. So, years passed with nobody ever having viewed any of his works set up in any gallery. He thought judgment was there anyway. One evening, after a discussion with a friend who inspired him to be bold, he called up a small gallery space to hold a modest exhibition.

In preparation, Liam started sharing his artwork on social media small steps that made his perspective change accordingly. With every like and encouraging comment, he reduced his fear and started converting it into excitement. The day of the exhibition came when he was standing in front of an audience and was full of anxiety; he chose to breathe through it. But as he spoke about his passion, Liam discovered that vulnerability could coexist with strength. His fear was met not with criticism but with admiration, a reality he once thought impossible.

Exercises & Reflective Questions: Taking Small Steps

Exercise: Fear Inventory

Start by writing three things that feel overwhelming to you.
Next to each item, write down what you think when you
see or hear that thing. Next week, pick one to focus on
every day. Think of what actions, no matter how small, you
can take to do something to defeat the fear.

Reflective Question:

What do you believe underlies your fears? What binding
factors might those beliefs offer? Are they born out of
truth or perception? Take some quiet time and discover
how these beliefs control your behavior.

Healing Moment: Visualization

Close your eyes and breathe in and out a few times.
Remember one place that feels safe for you. Now, with
these deep breaths, envision being there with your fear
standing in front of you. You can see how you would take
the steps to overcome it, hearing the voice within you
guide you through this process. Allow yourself to take in
the shift from fear to empowerment.

Cinematic Approach: Your Life as a Hero's Journey

Envision yourself as the hero of your epic story. You
become trapped in the opening scene with fear,
uncertainty, and restraint. The catalyst comes when a
mentor figure meets you it might be a friend, a book, or a
moment of introspection. They present to you the

challenge to face your fears step by step. As the story unfolds, you begin walking through your fears, one small step at a time, and it reveals your strength. You stand victorious, not because the fear vanished, but because you learned to dance with it, wrapped in your courage.

Conversations of Change: A Dialogue on Fear

Riya: "You know, I never really realized how paralyzing fear could be until I had to face it head on. What was your experience with it?"

Kiran: "For me, it was like a dark cloud hanging over my head. I thought that avoiding it was the answer. But every time I ran, that cloud grew bigger."

Riya: "Exactly! Until then, I had learned that facing it, even in small doses, was the true key to liberation."

Kiran: "One of the best things I did was journal my fears. Just writing them down felt like shedding their power somehow."

Riya: "That is kind of crucial, isn't it? Our minds can warp reality, making them feel impossible to confront. With words, we begin to look at them for what they are."

Kiran: "Absolutely. And victory over little things creates that momentum. Fear is a great teacher."

As their discussion progresses, both Riya and Kiran come to the empowering realization that gradual exposure to the feared thing reduces its weight, shifting from a stepped giant to a stepping stone toward a brighter future.

Gradual Exposure to Fears: A Message of Motivation

Let's agree on this undeniable truth: fear will always be part of life. But it never has to dictate our narrative. Gradual exposure to our fears enables us to reclaim our power, rewrite our stories, and redefine who we are in the light of courage. Remember, transformation doesn't demand a giant leap; it begins with the smallest of steps.

Therapeutic Approach & Healing Moment: Restorative Shift

Therapeutic Moment:

Sit comfortably and close your eyes. Bring forward a fear that feels very heavy for you. What is it, and what does that look like? What are you experiencing in relation to that fear? With each exhale, imagine letting this fear go. Visualize it floating out into the air. Now imagine that life without it is possible and how free you can be. Accept the clarity this release brings to you and feel peace wash over you.

Final Thought: Your Journey, Your Power

The path is personal, and every little step reveals layers you never knew existed within yourself. You see, this power to change how you relate to fear is within you. Cultivate a mindset of courage and resilience, and you create a reality where fear no longer strangles but becomes an ally.

Reflection Prompt/Closing Thoughts:

As you begin this fearless journey, take a moment to reflect on:

- What fears have held you back, and how would your life change by facing them?
- Can you identify one small action you can take this week to work against your fears?
- Picture living every day with courage. What does that look and feel like for you?

The experience of gradually overcoming fears starts in the mind, and it is your choice to support the realization of a world filled with courage and potential.

Chapter 4: Nurturing Mental Well-being through Health and Fitness

Introduction:

Our physical and mental well-being are very intertwined; the basis of a well-rounded life starts with care of both. This chapter discusses how health and fitness play an integral part in maintaining mental well-being. Understanding the mind-body relationship, we will explain the importance of exercise, nutritious eating, and adequate rest for not only strengthening your body but for sharpening your mind and providing mental toughness. By establishing an exercise routine that is not overly taxing, we could have a solid foundation set in place for mental health that will help us come alive in all aspects. So, let's look into how this simple practice can lead to a more harmonic, energized, and satisfied mind.

4.1) The Body Connection and Its Impact on Health

Introduction: The Mind-Body Connection

Imagine that a delicate dance is taking place in your mind. Your thoughts lead, and your body follows harmoniously. The mind and the body do not exist in isolation but are interdependent, with impacts that intricately shape each other. What if I realized that the quality of my mental health directly correlates with my physical well-being? This relationship, complicated and profound, is not just theoretical; it is actually a basic principle that can change everything you know about health.

Every anxious thought and each happy moment resonate through the body a symphony that lifts you up or weighs you down.

Quotes: Echoes of Wisdom

- *"The mind is like water. When it's turbulent, it's hard to see. When it's calmed, everything becomes clear." — Prasad Mahes"*
- *What we think, we become; what we feel, we attract; what we imagine, we create." — Christian D. Larson"*
- *Mental health is not a destination but a process. It's about how you drive, not where you're going." — Noam Shpancer*

These profound quotes remind us that our mental state is a catalyst for our physical reality. They show us how we must nurture our thoughts and emotions, all of which create ripples in our physical health.

Poem: A Tapestry Unraveled

"In whispers of thought, the body feels.

Our well-being linked, like spinning wheels.

A flicker of joy or waves of despair,

Each pulse of feeling, a thread we share.

Mind and body, a story woven together,

Where heartbeats resonate, spirit with the weather.

Stilled breath brings our way;

Healing unfurls in the light of day.:"

This is some pretty deep level mind-body play on how the human emotional topography can find a way to guide itself in the very fabric of our bodies, reminding us that mental health is the basis for being well.

Relatable Stories: Waking Up to Awareness

Consider the case of James, a man who spent years struggling with chronic pain. Doctors could find no physical explanation for his suffering, yet his everyday struggle was so overwhelming that something had to give. In this case, he desperately sought guidance from a holistic therapist who put him squarely in touch with the mind-body connection. "Your body is talking to you," she said. "What are your thoughts telling you?"

He started to look into the layers of emotions that were actually supporting his pain. He found feelings of not being good enough and fear. Through exercises in mindfulness and deconstructing the negative beliefs he witnessed, he saw changes even in his pain. But most notably, throughout all walks of life, he realized that at his own slow, crawl pace, his body would begin to reflect this healing journey of the mind toward both physical and emotional liberation.

Exercises & Reflective Questions: The Acting Out Change

Exercise: Body Scan Meditation

Find a quiet space and do a body scan meditation. Focus your awareness, from the tips of your toes to the top of your head bringing attention to each part of your body. Notice where there is tension or discomfort. Reflect on thoughts that may be contributing to these sensations, and breathe them out, being conscious of releasing tension as you exhale.

Reflective Questions:

- When you feel anxious or stressed, how do you notice these emotions manifesting in your body?

- What patterns can you identify between your emotional experiences and the sensations in your body?

Healing Moment:

Close your eyes. Recall a moment when you were fully comfortable. What thoughts were present in that moment? How did your body react? Now imagine bringing that ease back into today, inviting it in so your mind and body can both find calm and renewal together.

Cinematic Method: Your Story of Change

Imagine yourself as the hero in a makeover movie. In the beginning, you're burdened by inner conflicts. It then proceeds with the score playing a melancholic tune that reflects the inner fight. A wise character then appears; this may be a mentor, a book, or an epiphany that opens up enlightenment regarding the body connection. The music changes to indicate that this is a different tone. You listen and align your thoughts with self-love and acceptance. The camera zooms in on you as you face challenges, noticing the physical responses to every thought. You leave the cinema empowered at the end, proving to yourself that your story is, after all, a tapestry of emotional and physical resilience woven into it.

Conversations of Change: A Podcast Dialogue

Voices of Healing: A Journey

Join Alex and hear him share his reflections on personal experiences involving the powerful interplay between the mind and body.

Alex: "Today, I want to share something really profound. Our mental and physical health is not two different things; they are connected. At a certain point in time, I used to ignore this connection, believing that my mind could be separated from my body."

"I remember when stress consumed my life. My body experienced fatigue, headaches, and muscle tension. Then I learned to pay attention to those connections. I started practicing yoga and mindfulness. All of a sudden, those very bodily symptoms became a form of communication and an invitation to listen to myself."

And the truth we must hold close to our hearts is that the inner dialogue forms the external world around us. Every thought carries weight, and each is capable of healing or harming. So, I ask that we reflect on this: What stories are you telling your body? Are they stories that empower you or drag you down?"

This is where our conversations between our minds and our bodies receive some good fresh air; astonishing transformation is ahead. It's not about freedom from struggles, but rather a matter of awareness regarding how these struggles affect our health."

The Power of Connection: A Motivational Message

The connection between mind and body reminds us that mental health is just as important as physical health. It underscores the need to take care of both holistically. When we cultivate our well-being, we bestow our bodies with the gift of healing. Knowing the strong bond between the two empowers us to make conscious choices that enhance our overall health, opening up the door to life at its best.

Therapeutic Approach & Healing Moment: Guided Shift

Therapeutic Moment:

Take a moment. Close your eyes and reflect on how you felt out of balance. Perhaps it was during a time of stress or anxiety. Reflect on the thoughts your mind produced. Were they filled with doubt or fear? Let them go gently and make space for declarations of strength and peace. Replace those thoughts with empowering beliefs: "I am whole. I am healed." Feel the healing sensations overcome you, knowing that real healing includes the mind.

Final Thought: Align with Your Inner Harmony

It is through the recognition of that connection that an individual embarks on the path of mental and physical well-being. Each thought can either be a brick for building resilience or an obstacle to moving forward. When consciousness is nurtured, attended to, and provided for, as one develops a positive attitude, the ability to knit together a golden thread woven of wellness is discovered, one that symbolizes living a life of health, happiness, and fulfillment.

Reflection Prompt/Closing Thoughts

Reflect on the following as you continue your journey of discovering the mind-body connection:

- How deeply do you understand the relationship between your thoughts and your physical health?
- What small changes might you make in your daily routine to foster a healthier balance between both?
- How would you transform if you embraced the innate wisdom of your body and mind?

Healing begins within: an inner landscape grows into a deep and profound connection, assuming the beauty of both mind and body at their brightest.

4.2) Introduction to Physical Wellness Practices: Exercise, Nutrition, and Sleep

Introduction: Shaping the Wellness Within

Imagine waking up each morning refreshed and reenergized. What if I told you this state of being is a result of mindful techniques you can incorporate into your life? Physical wellness refers to a harmonious integration of exercise, nutrition, and sleep, three interdependent pillars that support not only the body but also the mind. The actions taken in nurturing your physical health weave the fabric of your overall vitality.

Quotes: Wisdom for the Wellness Journey

- *"It is health that is real wealth, and not pieces of gold and silver." — Mahatma Gandhi"*
- *"Take care of your body. It's the only place you have to live." — Jim Rohn."*
- *"It is the only place you have to live. Live well, because you are there. Each and every moment matters." — Jim Rohn*
- *"Your body is a temple, but only if you treat it as one." — Astrid Alauda*

These words gently remind us that our wellness must be cared for by ourselves in a very sacred commitment. In this context, taking care of our bodies prepares the foundation for a successful life.

Poem: Symphony of Self-Care

"In morning light, we start our day,

With exercise, our souls renew at play.

Food artfully cooked in colors so fine,

Every mouthful takes us to the sky.

Rest softly, like a balm that brings ease;

In sleep, our hearts find a peaceful release.

Thus, these are the same elements a waltz of grace,

That steers us to our proper place."

This poem represents the interaction of exercise, nutrition, and sleep for the betterment of overall wellness. Each ingredient contributes to a holistic lifestyle that promotes physical as well as mental health.

Related Stories: Transformative Journeys

Imagine the story of Mark, a man whose life revolved around work, more work, and fast food. A succession of years where he did so, imagining that its price devotion could only better show off his diligence and ambition. He soon felt its cost: fatigue, lethargy, and a sense of discontentment that never went away.

One day, Mark encountered a local wellness workshop that dramatized exercise, nutrition, and sleep. Inspired by these testaments, he decided to take the leap. He started allocating his time to regular walks, testing boulder whole foods, and establishing a firm sleep schedule. Gradually, he experienced refreshing swings in energy and viewpoint as his body began to respond to the change. The world, once weighed down by burdens, became an exciting tapestry of real possibilities.

Exercises & Reflective Questions: Building Wellness Awareness

Exercise: Daily Wellness Journal

Record your daily habits of exercise, nutrition, and sleep for a week. What decisions did you make? How did these practices affect your mood and energy? Think about patterns and shifts as the days go by.

Reflective Questions:

- Of these three areas exercise, nutrition, and sleep which do you think is the most neglected in terms of your lifestyle today?
- What's one small change you can make today to help foster improvement?

Healing Moment:

Close your eyes and breathe in deeply. Imagine your body pulsating with vital energy. Think about how each of these wellness habits exercise, nutrition, and sleep contributes to this picture of harmony. Feel all the rejuvenation flowing through your body. What does this vision look like for you in your life today?

Cinematic Approach: Your Journey to Wellness

Imagine you are one of the protagonists in a story of change. You are in Act One, weighed down by bad habits and overwhelmed by them. The plot changes when you meet with a mentor; it may be the nutritionist, the fitness coach, or an inspiring book, which shows you the path to wellness. As you engage in exercise, nourishing food, and restorative sleep, the cameras follow your journey.

Now you're overcoming obstacles in strength filming scenes of colorful meals, invigorating workouts, and peaceful nights. In the final scene, you discover an element of yourself you never would have imagined was possible: all energy, thriving, and most certainly alive. Your journey toward wellness has rewritten your story.

Conversations of Change: A Panel Discussion on Wellness

The Wellness Shift: A Conversation about bodily health

Join our lively conversation with Sarah, Tom, Emily, and Alex as we discuss the key elements of physical well-being.

Sarah: "So today, let's discuss how physical behaviors, such as exercise, nutrition, and sleep, can affect overall health. Tom, why do you think your bodily choices matter so much?"

Tom: "When we value these ingredients, we feel better, and we work better at everything we do."

Emily: "Absolutely. Food is our fuel; it's how we can think clearly and maintain energy. Making mindful choices can change our entire outlook."

Alex: "And let's not forget to sleep! It's our body's time to recharge and recover. No amount of exercise in the world will help you if you're not getting proper sleep."

Sarah: "What concrete suggestions do you have for those who are experiencing this?"

Tom: "Take it one step at a time. Find something that you enjoy doing physically and make it a habit."

Emily: "Try to cook at home. Find new vegetables and ingredients you like and see what balances you best."

Alex: "Develop a nighttime ritual. Make sure you're unwinding and take sleep seriously."

Sarah: "Great advice!"

A conscious approach to wellness will bring drastic changes.

Wellness is not a destination; it is a journey taken together.

The Power of the Mind: A Motivational Message

As you walk your wellness path, the truth you'll discover is that your physical health is a part of your mindset. How you see exercise, nutrition, and sleep can have a significant influence on how well you can stick to the plan. Changing your mindset allows you to see wellness not as a chore but as a path to even more fun and vibrancy in living.

Therapeutic Approach & Healing Moment: The Guided Shift

Therapeutic Moment:

Breathe in deeply. With your eyes closed, recall a time you felt truly alive and comfortable. What were your choices then? Allow yourself to bring back those sensations of energy and clarity. Breathe out with each exhale any limiting beliefs that tell you wellness is impossible. On the contrary, embrace the thought of subtle repeated choices leading to grand metamorphosis.

Final Thought: Your Road to Wellness

The door to physiological health opens through the purposeful actions that you place in your life. Each intentional decision you make walking, consuming nutritious whole foods, or enjoying rejuvenating sleep builds a cascade of ripples toward a more vibrant life experience. The more aware you become of your habits and orient them toward wellness, the more reality you begin to construct reflecting your very vitality.

Reflective Prompt/Closing Thoughts:

For the final time, take some time to reflect on your journey to wellness. Do not forget to ask yourself these questions:

- How attentive are you to your own body's practices?
- What small, actionable thing might you do today to enhance wellness?
- How would it feel to live a life anchored in health and vitality every day?

Your path to physical well-being is precious. Embrace that gift with love, intent, and mindfulness to nourish your body and enable it to be the spirited performer it is in this beautiful dance of life.

4.3) Balanced Health Routine Strategies That Promote Mental Well-being

Introduction: The Interplay of Body and Mind

Imagine a life where your body health is amazingly intertwined with your mental well-being. What if you thought of your body and mind as partners in a daily journey, each playing a significant role in helping the other? Not only do routines fulfill our physical needs, but they also serve as the scaffolding for a healthy mental state to grow upon. You can begin a journey of transformation by establishing a balanced health routine, which will open doors to well-being and happiness.

Quotes: Wisdom That Speaks

- *"It is health that is real wealth and not pieces of gold and silver." — Mahatma Gandhi"*
- *The mind and body are not separate. What affects one, affects the other." — Hippocrates"*
- *Take care to get what you like, or you will be forced to like what you get." — George Bernard Shaw*

These thoughtful reflections prompt us to understand that a healthy life is holistic in its pursuit, that is, when body and mind are nourished, so is life itself. In the perfect balance of these two forces, it is as though a ray of light pours down upon the long path toward profound wellness.

Poem: Bridging Wellness

"In life's pace, with every step we take,

Body and mind in a delicate wake.

Nourish your soul, let it flow

In the rhythm of harmony, watch your garden grow.

Balance the scales, let energies meet;

In every heartbeat, the rhythm is so sweet.

As you tend to health, let kindness flow,

Admit laughter and tears."

This poem reminds us that physical health and mental clarity go hand in hand. Thus, it demands nurturing of both aspects to eventually create a life that feels complete and rewarding.

Related Stories: The Adventure of Grace

Consider Grace, for example. She was a woman caught in the downward spiral of modern life. Much office pressure, along with work and personal obligations, drained her mentally and left her utterly exhausted. One morning, while juggling all this and feeling overwhelmed and fatigued, she ran into a mindful health coach. "How about you treat your body as a temple and your mind as its guiding light?" the coach asked.

Intrigued but skeptical, Grace decided to experiment. She added short morning walks to wake up her body and mindful breathing exercises to calm her thoughts. Slowly, she noticed a shift; her anxiety was washed away, her energy surged, and her days were filled with vibrancy she hadn't experienced in years. Layering movement, mindfulness, and nutrition transformed the mundane aspects of her routine into a sanctuary for the body and mind.

Exercises & Reflective Questions: Building Harmony

Exercise: Conscious Movement

15 minutes per day moving in a way that delights you. Maybe it's practicing yoga, dancing, walking in the woods, or simply stretching over your desk. Pay attention to how your body feels in these, and the clarity that arrives with conscious movement.

Reflective Question:

What time of day do you connect with your body? In what ways does this awareness impact your mental space?

Healing Moment:

Sit comfortably with your eyes closed; visualize a day when you fully embrace balance. Keep recalling the moments when you nurtured both your body and mind. Let that energy light up and fill you with warmth and positivity.

Cinematic Approach: Your Life as a Wellness Journey

Imagine your life as a colorful film where you are not only a passive observer but the protagonist who actively moves through a health story. At first, the movie is a shaggy tale of routines gone wild, bewilderment, and disjointed living. Then comes the plot twist: the realization of the importance of balance; a mentor, some book or moment of clarity propels you to rethink your lifestyle.

As the scenes unfold, you beautifully weave wellness into your daily narrative. Every act highlights the key moments of living with healthy food, exercise, and clearer thoughts. By the final scene, you find yourself standing tall, full of health and joy, a glorious expression of a well-told story of balance.

Dialogues of Change: Podcast Conversation

The Wellness Spectrum: A Conversation with Marcus and Liz

Let's wade into a conversation about the relationship between health and well-being of the mind.

Marcus: "Liz, isn't it fascinating how your health regimes bleed into your psychological mode of living? I have seen firsthand how exercise has an elevating effect on mood. What has been your experience?"

Liz: "Absolutely, Marcus. There was a time when I neglected movement, and it showed. When I started including brisk walks in my routine, I could almost feel my mood lift several notches. It's as if each step released a weight."

Marcus: "That's a powerful illustration. So, have you noticed other shifts in your life since prioritizing your health?"

Liz: "Absolutely! Supporting my body through good nutrition has created this beautiful relationship where I want to eat healthy food, which in turn fuels my energy and mental clarity. It's just beautiful."

Marcus: "What advice would you give to someone just starting his or her journey toward better balance?"

Liz: "Start small. Choose one area whether it's enriching your diet, adding a few minutes of movement, or practicing mindfulness. Small changes aggregate into significant transformations."

As this conversation unfolds, both Marcus and Liz highlight the essence of nurturing our health, reminding listeners that each small step leads to greater harmony in life.

The Power of Mindset: A Motivational Message

Here lies the truth: your well-being depends on both your physical and mental health. Each small act to achieve this balance enriches your experience and radiates positivity throughout life. By growing in this middle ground, you nurture a haven that increases your ability to bounce back from ebbs and flows. Remember that every step taken to foster health harbors strength for the mind.

Therapeutic Approach & Healing Moment: Guided Shift

Therapeutic Moment:

Take a breath in; breathe out softly. Close your eyes and visualize a time when you felt exhausted, wandering in a haze of fatigue. Observe what you thought about yourself back then. Now, gently let go of those words and envision a new story: Instead of telling yourself, "I don't have time," tell yourself, "I honor my self-care." Let this new mantra wash over you, bringing you a feeling of empowerment and inner peace.

Final Thoughts: Your Path to Well-Being

The path to whole health is a lifelong journey of self and inner development. Every intentional action taken benefits your being as a whole. Awareness and dedication can then become the keys that open the door to the possibility of a vibrant, meaningful life, one that honors not only the vessel but also the mind.

Reflection Prompt/Closing Thoughts:

- How does your current routine reflect your holistic health goals?
- What would it mean for you to honor both your body and mind daily?
- How might small, deliberate actions create noteworthy shifts in your well-being?

Your health journey is a narrative waiting to be written. Let every thought and every small choice cultivate a beautiful story of balance and fulfillment.

Chapter 5: Cultivating Love and Meaningful Connections

Introduction:

It's as if the relationships that flow into our lives are the lifeline of human existence and shape the emotional and mental landscapes profoundly. Love, friendship, or community relations can give meaning and significance to one's life by bringing enormous joy and fulfillment. Yet, creating and maintaining such meaningful relationships calls for hard work, mutual understanding, and a sense of vulnerability. This chapter explores the art of cultivating relationships that not only are fulfilling but are transformative connections that help us grow, heal, and navigate life's challenges with grace and strength.

5.1) Components of Healthy, Trusting Relationships

Introduction: Connection, Laying the Bridge of Trust

Imagine relationships like a bridge between two people, weaving together experiences, feelings, and aspirations. It is built with trust as its foundation; otherwise, the connection remains fragile, with the threat of tides of misunderstanding and conflict sweeping it away. Do you see that in every moment, every exchange lies the possibility to cement this very thread? Trust is not something you give your hand so lightly; it's made by consistency, vulnerability, and open dialogue.

Quotes: Gems of Wisdom

- *"It is trust that transforms a group of people into a team."* — *Simon Sinek"*
- *"Trust is built with consistency." — Lincoln Chafee"*
- *"To be trusted is a greater compliment than being loved."* — *George MacDonald*

These quotes show us the very foundation of trust in any given relationship. They remind us that trust is not just a word but an alive commitment, built by actions and shared experiences.

Poem: The Dance of Connection

"In the dance of two hearts entwined,

Trust is the whisper that can be defined.

Nurtured through kindness, respect, and care,

An unbroken bond, and truth to share.

With each promise kept, with every sigh,

Connection strengthens, on high.

In the tapestry of souls, trust weaves its thread,

Creating a haven where love is spread."

This poem makes easy sense: Trust loves and is loved in return. It's how kindness, respect, and authenticity gradually weave a tapestry to hold two people together.

Relevant Case Study: The Revival of Trust

Imagine James and Ella, who have just reached the crossroads in their relationship. All the communication has dwindled, bringing along misunderstandings and distancing themselves from one another. One evening, during a very candid conversation, Ella finally said, "I can't feel you here anymore. We need to rebuild our trust."

Being alert to the cracks that have started forming, he agreed to vulnerability. The two hugged each other and shared their inadequacy fears before listening as Ella spoke about hers. Honest dialogue led them to realize that healing their emotional gap came through intentional endeavors: weekly check-ins, appreciation of efforts, and showing gratitude. As they began to prioritize their connection, their relationship flourished into a deep-rooted sense of security and trust.

Exercises & Reflective Questions: Building Trust

Trust Circles

Sitting together, create a "trust circle" in which you and others share aspirations and fears. Establish a space in which vulnerability is encouraged; use active listening practices so that both voices are heard.

Reflective Question:

- How do I show trust in my relationships?
- Are there areas where I can cultivate deeper openness?

Healing Moment:

Close your eyes and take a deep breath. Recall a moment in which trust was established or lost. Describe what you felt. How did this experience inform your relationship afterward? Envision a climate of trust and openness, hearts unguarded and vulnerable. What can you do to get closer to that vision?

Cinematic Approach: Your Love Story

Imagine you are a film director, creating a heartbreak movie about relationships. The opening scene unifies parts of misgivings and fears when characters are introduced, and the issue of a lack of genuine communication is brought out and pursued. Friends guide the protagonists on their journey to reestablish trust as they reflect on themselves and aspire to find mutual understanding.

They talk about such fears between each other, confronted with their biggest weaknesses, and pave the way for an emotional breakthrough toward healing. This final act has made for a completely different relationship: laughing, respectful, and filled with seamless trust. Thus, rebuilding is actually possible through intention and connection.

Conversations of Change: Podcast Dialogue

Connecting Hearts: Dialogue with Mia

Join Mia as she explores with you the real heart of what trust is about in relationships.

Mia: "Today, I want to share with you, on the basis of a good relationship, trust. It's that invisible force that makes us feel safe to be together. So, how do we build it?"

I recall a friend, Lila, who had some issues in a long-term relationship. At the start, little weekly reflections of gratitude and vulnerability ensued. Overnight, conversations bloomed into better understanding, compassion, and respect. Through intention, they carved their way toward rebuilding trust."

Trust essentially means performing what we promise. Every promise we fulfill constructs a foundation that stands firm against any raging storm. So, what stories are you telling each other? Are you weaving together a narrative of trust or uncertainty?

In her concluding remarks, Mia nudges listeners into reflection on their relationships: "Every moment presents an opportunity for growth, and the foundation of trust can be the greatest catalyst for connection. How will you choose to nurture trust today?"

The Heart of Trust: Inspirational Message

If there is one thing that certainty says through relationships, it's that trust is the pulse of connection. It makes us feel safe to be open, to share the honesty of who we are, and to let go and be ourselves in each other's presence. As we intentionally grow our trust, deepen our understanding, and open ourselves up to vulnerability, we uncover deeper layers of emotional intimacy.

As you look inward at your relationships, remember that change starts with you. Every choice to act with integrity and respect strengthens the ties between us, creating a safe haven in which love can grow.

Therapeutic Approach & Healing Moment: The Gentle Turning Point

Therapeutic Moment:

Breathe deeply. Close your eyes and remember a moment when trust was broken. Identify the feelings in that moment: fear, hurt, betrayal? Now imagine a shift: replace those feelings with compassion and understanding not only for the other person but also for yourself. Rebuild trust. Maybe it's the verbal talk, the committed actions, or just giving grace in order to heal. Let this healing and connection overflow from this moment into your heart. Recognize how much capacity you have for growth.

Final Thought: Trust as Your Superpower

Trust is an incredible gift: the ability to reshape your relationships in deep, profound ways. Each one of your interactions provides an opportunity to deepen this vital bond.

A lived understanding of how you communicate, living up to your agreements, and being vulnerable helps create a world filled with connection and relationship.

Reflection Prompt/Closing Thoughts:

As you walk through your relationships, take pause to reflect on the following:

- How do your actions and words contribute to the trust you build with others?
- What small changes could you initiate to deepen the trust in your connections?
- How would it feel to fully embrace vulnerability and openness, nurturing trust as a foundation for profound relationships?

So, here's the start of your journey to healthy and trusting relationships: one step in nurturing trust within yourself and extending that to others around you.

5.2) Effective Communication Skills that Emphasize Empathy and Understanding

Introduction: Unite Hearts and Minds

Imagine a world where every conversation sparks not only dialogue but connection. A space where words break free from their literal meanings and inject sparks of empathy and understanding into each communication. What if, with just a few conscious changes in how we communicate, we could break the trend of our interactions? To build those bridges and dissolve those barriers, we must "connect" through our own ways of communication. The words we choose to express ourselves form the foundation of our connections and influence how we interpret the world around us.

Quotes: Glimpses of Understanding

- *"The greatest problem in communication is the illusion that it has been accomplished." - George Bernard Shaw"*
- *"Communication works for those who work at it." — John Powell"*
- *"Empathy is about finding echoes of another person in yourself." — Mohsin Hamid*

These thoughts remind us that communication is an art, a subtle play of words and emotions that goes far beyond swapping mere words. They reveal a salient fact: empathy and understanding begin with our ability and willingness to genuinely connect with other people.

Poem: The Language of Connection

"Whispered soft, or clear voices say,

And empathy springs forth when we truly hear.

Not in the words, but feelings convey

Shared understanding opens hearts to share.

Communication weaves a tapestry so bright;

The strands of compassion shine light in the fight.

What we say and to whom we are connected can alter

The landscape of love, hope, and fate."

This poem describes the essence of empathy in communication, that is, the emotional resonance that truly effective exchanges can create. Honest listening and speaking bring an atmosphere full of potential to connect.

Credible Stories: Understanding Made Easy

Think of Max as he plunged into the choppy waters of his first job. Surrounding him is a panoply of coworkers' variety, racial, and cultural diversity. Frequently, he felt cut off as conversations swirled around him like leaves caught in the wind. Frustrated and dazed, Max went to his manager, Lisa, for guidance.

"Max, have you thought about how your communication could be influencing your relationships here?" she asked softly.

Instead of getting confused, he opted to observe. He learned how the colleagues shared their stories that hinted at their backgrounds, struggles, and aspirations. Inspired, he gradually began responding not only to words but to the emotions behind them, using open-ended and empathetic responses. As time went by, the atmosphere evolved from conversations to laughter and togetherness. Max learned that by embracing empathy, he was no longer only heard but truly understood.

Exercises & Reflective Questions: Cultivating Active Listening

Exercise: The Listening Walk

Pair up with a friend and take a walk. As you stroll, share your thoughts and feelings about a chosen topic. Concentrate on listening without interrupting, even for a moment. Reflect on the experience afterward, how did it feel to listen fully? Did it change how you engaged with your friend?

Reflective Questions:

- What do you do when someone starts to open up and share their story with you?

- Are you being an active listener, or are you waiting for your turn so you can begin talking about your response?

Healing Moment:

Close your eyes and take a few deep breaths. Recall the last time you had a conversation with someone that genuinely connected. What elements made that exchange special? Now envision how you can infuse more of that into your future dialogues, going much deeper than before.

Cinematic Approach: The Story of Your Life in Dialogue

Consider your life as an intricately woven film. You sit in a colorful café, surrounded by many types of characters. The camera zooms in on a conversation that starts off casual but, beneath the surface, reveals a desire for understanding. At the peak of the conversation, you put away your phone, lean forward, and really listen to the teller of the tale. Feelings are exposed, and suddenly the air changes. The story unfolds into one of embracing human connection as sympathy weaves in with each spoken word. You then recognize that such a small act of connecting has enhanced your life and strengthened all the relationships you share.

Conversations of Change: A Podcast Dialogue

The Art of Communication: A Conversation between Ava and Leo

Join Ava and Leo as they explore the subtleties of empathy and the art of listening within conversation.

Ava: "Leo, communication to me is not just about the words. It's how we make others feel in that one moment. Can you recall a time you felt really heard?"

Leo: "Absolutely, Ava. I remember one day when a friend listened in a non-judgmental way. That really made me realize how powerful it is to create that space for someone. It's like we got into harmony."

Ava: "So true! And how can you nurture that and create more of it in everyday interactions?"

Leo: "Because I am here. When we listen, we allow the other person to be open. In itself, it makes the dialogue something important."

Ava: "Exactly, because it is a dance of connection, isn't it? Every type of connection has within itself the possibility of being a stepping stone to deep understanding."

As they conclude their conversation, Ava and Leo leave the listeners with an important message: every conversation can be a chance for empathy, creating a world of deep understanding.

The Power of Empathy: A Motivational Message

The very core of human bonding lies in the extraordinary ability to empathize. Empathy is the ability to understand and share others' feelings, and such understanding opens the door to a relationship that is truly transformational. Conscious honing of our communication skills births environments that nurture compassion, patience, and harmony.

Remember: growth comes from simple acts; it will bloom even more when we choose to listen, comprehend, and connect. In other words, carefully chosen words can change the course.

Therapeutic Approach & Healing Moment: A Guided Shift

Therapeutic Moment:

Breathe in. Close your eyes, and recall the most recent conversation that left you drained. What was going through your head as the other person talked to you? Let the judgment go. Now envision the conversation differently. What if your focus had been on understanding? Let this shift within you bring about peace and connection. As you see the potential for deeper relationships in this new narrative, play it out: continue.

Final Thoughts: Your Empathic Potential

You and I have the ability to enhance empathy and understanding by simply talking. Every word we choose to say and every ear we lend may either build walls or bridges.

By intentionally focusing on our style of communication and cultivating listening skills, we further open our hearts to richer and more meaningful connections.

Reflection Prompt/Closing Thoughts:

Take a minute to reflect on your journey:

- How often are you in conversation, really engaged in exchanges of understanding, rather than just reporting information?
- What small moves would facilitate more meaningful conversations?
- How would it feel to enter every discussion with the goal of building empathy and connection?

Words have such fantastic and enormous potential. Caringly nourished with empathy towards others' perspectives, they can truly become a reality of what they were destined to understand, to grow, and ultimately, to create real relationships.

5.3) Conflict Resolution Techniques and Building Greater Connections

Introduction: The Art of Connection

Conflict is; it's part of human connection. imagine, though, approaching conflict as a chance to deepen human connection versus being an insurmountable setback. What if the ultimate way to find resolution is a stroke that could enhance the canvas of your relationships? Every argument, if approached with care and deliberation, holds the potential for a stepping stone toward understanding and compassion. That is the real transformative power of conflict resolution: it is in the unraveling, not the result, of what's hidden within the ties that bind us together.

Quotes: Gems of Wisdom

- *"The biggest battles are fought within." - Garth Brooks*
- *"Conflict cannot survive without your participation." — Wayne Dyer*
- *"In the midst of chaos, there is also opportunity." — Sun Tzu*

Such quotes encourage reflection on the very nature of conflict. Resolution is not so much the active breaking down of disagreement as it is a cultivating of understanding because it's only through conflicts that we find meaningful clarifications and richer insights into our relationships.

Poems: The Dance of Dialogue

"In the shadows made by words unspoken,

The heart whispers secrets, sometimes soft and awful.

Through conflict's dance, a rhythm unfolds.

In the embrace of truth, new stories are told.

With open hearts, we navigate the storm.

In understanding's light, connections take form.

From discord's ashes, a new trust can rise.

In every war, there's a connection."

This poem encompasses the intricacy of the resolution of conflict. It proclaims the possibility within discord and embraces dialogue as the pathway to going deeper into understanding where connection blooms, even when it's hard.

Connected Stories: The Art of Listening

Let's take the case of Mark and Sarah. Best friends since college days, they eventually ended up in an argument over what seemed like a petty matter. As both grew more irate, their bond started to fray. One night, sitting closer to each other, Mark said very softly, "I feel that nobody hears me and no one understands my perspective." Sarah sat there, silent. She knew this was a moment not to let go of the relationship. "I never meant that," she said. "Let's talk about what we both want in this."

They were able to resolve it by openly and honestly talking through issues, finally uncovering fears and insecurities that had driven them apart. By recognizing each other's feelings, they were not only resolving the issue but strengthening their connection, leaving the experience with renewed trust.

Exercises & Reflective Questions: Building Connection Exercises

Exercise: The Active Listening Challenge

Schedule some time to talk with the other person and listen attentively without feeling the need to respond. Let them talk about what feels right for them without interrupting them. Then communicate back what you think they said just to let them know that you heard them.

Reflective Question:

What emotions do you experience as you listen and do not try to respond?

Healing Moment:

Step out of the room to an empty space. Breathe in deeply and recall the latest argument. Think about what you felt and why the other person may have been motivated to do and say what they did. Let that greater awareness open the door to empathy.

Cinematic Method: Your Resolution Voyage

Imagine your life like a movie. Conflict brews within the opening scenes, be it a misunderstanding with a loved one or a dispute with a colleague. As the plot thickens, a trusted mentor or a pivotal experience emerges, clarifying the importance of connection. Characters learn to navigate their differences by engaging in conversations that spark empathy and healing. There is a deep and transforming effect on character and relationships within this final scene where conflict helps them learn to look into one another to create bonds that are stronger and more trusting.

Conversations of Change: A Podcast Dialogue

Navigating Conflict: A Conversation with Liam and Sophia

Liam: "Conflict is the storm, isn't it, Sophia? How have you taken care of it in your relationships?"

Sophia: "Absolutely, Liam. I used to think of conflict as something to steer around, but now I view it as an opportunity. It came to me at my moment of truth when I realized every fight has the potential to be growth."

Liam: "That's really insightful. Can you share an example that illustrates this change?"

Sophia: "Absolutely! A friend and I fell out over differing views. Rather than holding on to resentment, we decided to meet up. I listened actively to her; her feelings were valid. By the end of the conversation, we forged not only a resolution but a deeper understanding of each other."

Liam: "That's beautiful. What advice would you give someone who is hesitant to confront conflict?"

Sophia: "Embrace vulnerability. Conflict is hard work, and it will make you better. Start small, and never forget that every conversation is an opportunity to develop a deeper connection."

The Power of Mindset: A Message of Resolution

Change begins with our attitude toward conflict. In that shift, seeing it as engaged and appreciated rather than avoided opens doors to connection. Every conflict challenges us to really know ourselves and others. As we learn to see conflicts as opportunities, the door to healing opens wide.

Therapeutic Approach & Healing Moment: Guided Reflection

Therapeutic Moment:

Take a minute to close your eyes and breathe deeply. Consider the last argument or misunderstanding. What were you or the other person afraid of or insecure about? Now, imagine a moment in which both people have truly been heard and considered. Visualize the conversation flowing with respect, mutual understanding, and renewed connection and trust.

Conclusion: The Connection Beyond Conflict

The skills of conflict resolution and relationship building are not just tools but rather strategies that make our lives richer. With empathy and open communication, we clear the paths toward understanding, binding us more intricately together as human beings. Each conflict resolved with intention will illuminate the depth of our relationships, shaping connections in ways that flourish over time.

Reflection Prompt/Closing Thoughts:

Reflect on these interactions as you go:

- How do you respond to disagreement?
- What are some practices that could help you better connect in moments of conflict?
- How might it feel to look at conflicts not as threats to your relationships but as opportunities for connection?

Awareness and grace in the navigation of conflict truly open the doors to significant growth, not only for you but for those surrounding you as well.

5.4) Significance of Community and Social Support Systems

Introduction: The Network of

Imagine a life where every challenge that comes your way
is met with a supportive hand, a listening ear, or a shared
laugh. Community isn't just the backdrop to our lives; it's a
tapestry of real human shared experiences, empathy, and
strength. What if you discovered that the strength you
most need to navigate the complexity of life is embedded
in those you touch? In those you rely on, you come to
understand that nobody is an island unto himself, with his
struggles, joys, and aspirations. The relationships that one
builds can greatly enhance mental and emotional
well-being as one navigates life with support and love.

Quotes: Words of Wisdom That Speak to the Heart

- *"Alone we can do so little; together we can do so much."*
  — Helen Keller
- *"It takes a village to raise a child." — African Proverb*
- *"The greatest gift of life is friendship, and I have received
  it." — Hubert H. Humphrey*

These words remind us, simply enough, that community is
the point. They urge us to recognize the truth that,
through another's uplift, we thrive, and highlight the
powerful interweaving of human experience.

Poem: Heart of Connection

"In the garden of life, we plant the seeds,

Water by kindness, shared hopes, and deeds.

Together we blossom, through laughter and tears;

In unity, we conquer doubt and fear.

When shadows fall heavy, and storms cloud our way,

There's a friend who brightens up the day.

In times of silence, laughter, and song,

Communities sing, belonging all around."

The poem captures the essence of community, showing how togetherness becomes a source of growth and comfort; therefore, it reinforces the realization that no journey is ever lonesome.

Relevant Stories: Tides of Support

We start with Liam, who floated on the tides of life. His career was stable, but isolation cast a gloom over a spirit that was once so bright. There, at a neighborhood gathering, he met Tara, who was full of warmth and energy. Through conversations about mutual interests, she drew him into a local group centered on personal development.

At first, he wasn't so sure, but it was then that Liam took the bold step of joining the group. In this community, vulnerability became strength, and with each story shared, he was reminded that he was not alone in anything, illuminating his path toward healing and growth. Encouraged by their support, he started taking risks that he had previously thought were too daunting. Not long after opening himself to the power of community, his life flourished in ways beyond what he ever would have surmised.

Exercises & Reflective Questions: Warming Up Our Ties

Exercise: Connection Journal

Commit to connecting with someone each day this week. It may be a friend, colleague, or acquaintance. Note how these connections make you feel and how they add value to your day. Share the threads of connection that you sense with these others.

Reflective Question:

- Who turns you around when times get tough?
- How can you deepen the connections or nurture new ones?

Healing Moment:

Close your eyes and take a few deep breaths. Think of a time when the community uplifted you during a challenge. What feelings arise when you think about that support? How could you seek or extend that type of support today?

Cinematic Approach: Your Community Story

Picture your life as a colorful film. You begin with lonely early scenes, hardly knowing how to navigate life's ups and downs. But now, entering this new chapter, the camera zooms in on this group of friends: the mentors, comrades, and cheerleaders that color your story. Inspiring through their laughter and encouragement, they set the spark in your journey. With teamwork, achieved goals, and love connecting you all together, situations come alive.

Climax: When these connections nurture the strength that conquers life's obstacles, the ending seems joyful, filled with reasons for being and belonging.

Conversations of Change: A Community Dialogue

Building Bridges: A Conversation on the Power of Community

Let's have an honest conversation with Maya, Khan, Leila, and Jamal about what community means to them.

Maya: "Community gives a sense of belonging, doesn't it? It enriches our lives in many ways that solitude cannot."

Khan: "Absolutely, Maya. I recall one specific instance when I felt so lost, but my community nudged me back. Oh man, it's amazing how the mere presence of people can change your outlook."

Leila: "And sometimes it has much to do with space; even a check-in or a shared meal speaks volumes about connection."

Jamal: "True. The smallest things, words, smiles, a fleeting display of weakness have the capacity to generate strong relationships."

Maya: "For those in the audience, what advice would you give to build a supportive community?"

Khan: "Be yourself first. Extend your hand. Sometimes just greeting someone gets the ball rolling toward making a close connection."

Leila: "Be open, be authentic. People are attracted to vulnerabilities."

Jamal: "And remember, community is reciprocal. Offer support when others need it, and it will come back to you."

Maya: "Beautifully said. Let us remind ourselves we all hold a part of the community quilt. When we invest in one another, we weave the beautiful tapestry of shared experience and strength."

The Strength of Community: A Motivational Reflection

One universal truth is clear: community is a lifeline. It's a connection that molds not only our mental and emotional states but also the perception of life itself. By nurturing those bonds, we can enrich our existence and the lives around us. Shared laughter, tears, and triumphs deepen our discovery that together we are stronger and can conquer seemingly insurmountable problems alone.

Therapeutic Approach & Healing Moment: Guided Embrace

Therapeutic Moment:

Breathe in, sensing the support of people around you friends, family, and even acquaintances. Recall a time when you were surrounded by love and encouragement. Acknowledge how this kind of support impacts your life. As you breathe out, imagine that you are sharing this warmth with others, knowing that giving and receiving is a fundamental aspect of community. Know that you are part of this precious mosaic called humanity.

Final Thought: Tapping Our Collective Potential

The source of strength for navigating the rough and smooth spots in life lies in the communities we build. Each intersection, each reach out in support lays a building block that coalesces into resilience and strength. You are actually designing the world you step into through the relationships you build that reflect your surroundings. Together, we can create a reality filled with hope, vibrancy, and endless possibility.

Reflection Prompt/Closing Thoughts:

The further you travel, take time to think about this:

- How actively are you engaging with your community?

- What must you do to create that feeling of connection in your life?
- How can the community help facilitate your empowerment journey and satisfaction?

The world around you is full of other people's lives. Celebrating these connections opens the door to a life richer in support, love, and growth.

Chapter 6: Understanding Psychology and Enhancing Mental Health

Introduction:

Our minds are intricate landscapes in which emotions, thoughts, and experiences carve their places. The more we comprehend the patterns of our psyche, the more clearly and purposefully we navigate our lives. This chapter brings us into the world of psychology, examining how your emotional patterns impact your actions and decisions. You will uncover real-life strategies for emotions regulation, stress management, and when needed, for support-an opportunity to delve deeper inside yourself and find mental wellness.

6.1) Emotional Patterns and Their Behavioral Implications

Introduction: The Psychological Landscape

Consider entering a room that is with all sorts of colors and textures, which further give way to arousing different emotions in you. As a painter uses various colors to create a masterpiece, similarly, your emotions from the reality of your experiences. Every feeling of joy, sadness, anger, or fear interines with your thoughts, generating emotional patterns that determine your behavior over time. Imagine waking up today and knowing that such patterns aren't just fleeting experiences but huge influences guiding your choices, responses, and interactions with the world.

Quotes: Enlightened Thoughts

- *"Feelings are just visitors; let them come and go." — Mooji*
- *"Emotion is the energy that shapes our experience of reality." — David R. Hawkins*
- *"It's not what happens to you, but how you react to it that matters." — Epictetus*

These words remind us that our emotions are not just spontaneous outbursts but are instead deeply patterned in those we continually engage with. They speak this fundamental truth: it is by knowing our emotions that we unlock the possibility to change our patterns and, therefore, our lives.

Poem: The Dance of Emotion

"The rhythm you feel, it softly beats,

Whispers of truth in your heart it greets.

Each pulse and wave, a story unfolds,

In the tapestry of life, your essence molds.

Emotions swell, wave crests rise,

They shape your moves and won't let you hide.

Those that you reach out to elevate,

Or strangle in the dark and stop the fire that beams."

This poem captures the subtle dance between emotion and behavior. It explains how the feelings one cultivates can either advance or dock one's path and how the latter determines which route to take.

Comparable Stories: Unfold Transformations

Consider the story of Jamie, an artist who had always felt she didn't really deserve her talent. The residuals of criticism that followed her throughout her life belied her image of brighter moments. She believed happiness was fleeting and that she would never belong. One day, in a flash of insight, she received a text from a friend: "What if you let yourself enjoy joy without guilt?"

She was skeptical at first but began to experiment with this concept. She started embracing her emotions; joy would wash over her without wondering whether or not it even existed. Slowly, she realized that the colors in her art were coming alive, the subjects were bolder, and the flow of her creative expression was pure and real. By actually recognizing her patterns of emotions, she changed her relationship with her art and, hence, her life.

Exercises & Reflective Questions: Cultivating Emotional Awareness

Exercise: Emotion Diary

For one week, maintain a diary to record your emotions each day. Note the context in which these feelings arise and how they influence your actions. Reflect on any patterns that emerge.

Reflective Questions:

When I am confronted with a stimulus that makes me emotional, what do I find myself responding with initially? Does this response align with how I would prefer to react?

Healing Moment:

Take a moment to settle comfortably. Take deep breaths and close your eyes. Recall an emotional response in the recent past that was overwhelming. What thoughts accompanied that feeling? Represent your release from limiting thoughts by embracing a kinder tale. How does this change the quality of your experience?

Cinematic Approach: Your Emotions as the Soundtrack

Imagine your life is a beautifully directed movie, where music underscores everything that's happening on the screen. Initially, the pieces of music are cacophonous, filled with dark notes of despair and uncertainty. Later, there is some turning point: a poignant conversation, a moment of silence, and the score becomes harmonious, illustrating new emotional strength. The difficulty you experience in your life is changing each emotional rub to subtly change the rhythm of the soundscape in the film. The last scenes are of a transformed character, thriving in the world, embracing the richness of his emotional patterns and how the narrative has come of age.

Conversations of Change: A Dialogue on Emotions

Reflections on Patterns: Alex's Solo Insight

Join Alex as they delve into the depth of emotional patterns and their implications for behavior.

Alex: "Let's discuss our emotions today. They're often considered just a passing moment, yet they are powerful undertows that guide our actions. Like the tide, they shape the landscape of our lives.

I recall a friend, Lisa, who couldn't stop feeling unworthy. Every failure simply drummed that belief into her: she couldn't cut it. One day, in some wide-open space, I asked her directly, 'What if your feelings are feedback, not facts?' This question began to change things.

She began to pay attention to her emotions, realizing they were guideposts, not facts. Gradually, she recalibrated her emotional responses, letting herself rejoice in accomplishments rather than tempering them. By shifting her perspective on her emotional patterns, she opened a whole world of possibility."

Life is a canvas where our emotions decide the strokes we write. Are you playing with bright colors or pastel shades? It all depends on how well you can understand and change your emotional patterns for yourself.

The Power of Emotional Awareness: A Motivational Message

Your emotions are a subtle force intricately interwoven in the fabric of your experiences. Realizing and knowing these emotional patterns gives you the fantastic power to influence your behavior and the course of your life. It's not an external change, but rather an internal recognition of what lies within. As you embark on this sojourn of emotional awareness, you open a new horizon of possibilities for yourself.

Therapeutic Approach & Healing Moment: Guided Reflection

Therapeutic Moment:

Close your eyes, breathe deeply, and recall the moment when you felt overwhelmed by negative thoughts. Allow those feelings to be there without judgment of yourself. Imagine the thoughts that accompanied them; were they founded upon fear or self-doubt? Let go of those thoughts slowly, opening room for a more empowering story. Maybe you start thinking, "I am resilient." Accept this new perception of yourself and let it surround you, changing the emotional topography and reality of your life.

Final Thought: The Inner Emotional Compass

Your emotions have the ability to command your life. Each feeling you encounter can either point you on the way to freedom or limit you to choices. By becoming responsible and aware of changing your emotional habits, you light up new pathways that become aligned with who you truly are. Remember, your feelings are not just feelings; they are the compass that steers you through the journey of life.

Reflection Prompt/Closing Thoughts:

The more deeply you observe your emotional patterns, consider the following:

- How often do you stop to watch the emotions that drive your behavior?
- What subtle shift in recognizing your emotional response could lead to some massive shifts in your behavior?
- How would it feel to move through the world with an honed awareness of your emotional landscape?

Your journey is a tapestry woven from your emotions. If you understand and tend to them, you embark on a profound journey of personal growth toward fulfilling realization.

6.2) Tools for Emotional Regulation and Stress Management

Introduction: Emotional Geography

Imagine painting a canvas where each brushstroke is an expression of your mind. Every feeling, ranging joy to sadness, anger, and confusion, adds emotion and color to an experience in life. What if, one day, the palette you had been working with became smeared and muddled by stress and turmoil? Emotional regulation is akin to learning to paint with a clear purpose. It involves awareness and intention, and, importantly, it provides the ability to deal with the complexities of life.

Quotes: The Wisdom of Reflection

- *"Emotions are the colors of the soul." — Wilhelm R. Bion"*
- *The greatest weapon against stress is our ability to choose one thought over another." — William James"*
- *When we are no longer able to change a situation, we are challenged to change ourselves." — Viktor Frankl*

These quotes remind us of the need to master our emotional states, as they inform us that how we approach stress impacts our well-being.

Poem: The Dance of Emotions

"In the storm of emotions, find your footing,

Breathe deep in the calmness, and let serenity.

Every wave of emotion is a lesson learned;

Through storms and through shadows, your spirit will burn.

Control gently, like the tide's ebb and flow;

Harness your feelings, and let positivity grow.

What you breed inside will certainly surface, as

A heart filled with equilibrium creates the best."

This poetic reflection presents the crux of emotional regulation while highlighting the need for developing inner balance in life's ebbs and flows.

Relevant Stories: Paths of Change

Let's imagine a young professional, Jack, drowning in anxiety. Every deadline was impossible; every decision felt like a disaster waiting to happen. His emotions swung between fierce determination and absolute fear. One day, in vulnerable confidence, he unpacked himself to a trusted friend with this insightful thought: "Emotions are messengers; we just need to learn how to listen."

Jack took it to heart. He started experimenting with ways he could handle his stress: mindfulness, meditation, and journaling. Gradually and incrementally, these tools changed his outlook. Instead of viewing his stressors as weights, he began tackling them as challenges that could be handled with dashing courage. Poised with newfound resilience, Jack faced life's forces with equilibrium, thereby opening himself up to progress.

Exercises & Reflective Questions: Developing Emotional Intelligence

Exercise: Emotional Check-In

Spend five minutes each day sitting still. Close your eyes and focus on the emotions that emerge. Label them without judgment. Are they heavy, light, anxious, or calm? This exercise builds emotional awareness and offers the first step toward regulation.

Reflective Questions:

What are you feeling during one of these stressful moments? How do you tend to react to those feelings? Do you think that's working?

Healing Moment:

Take a full breath, filling your lungs. Breathe out slowly, emptying out tension. Imagine a wave washing over you every breath clears; every exhalation lets go. Imagine you're buoyed up by the rhythm of your breathing.

Cinematic Approach: Working on Your Life Story

Picture your life as a film, where every scene represents another step in your emotional journey. The protagonist is you, and when the villainous stressors of life threaten to hijack the scene, a mentor comes in and introduces you to the mighty tools of emotional management. The camera focuses on your change as you breathe deeply; you focus your thoughts and anchor yourself in mindfulness. The climax portrays your victory in controlling stress to show the strength and elegance within you.

Conversations of Change: A Podcast Discussion

The Art of Emotional Regulation: A Discussion with Mia and David.

Mia: "David, it is astonishing how emotions can dominate our daily routines. Have you ever had times when stress became too much to handle?"

David: "Absolutely, Mia. I can recall a time when everything that was going on was making my anxiety worse. It was only with emotional regulation tools that I could start regaining control again."

Mia: "What were some of the tools that made the most difference for you?"

David: "Mindfulness meditation was a game changer. It allowed me to distance my emotions from my reactions. I began to observe rather than react."

Mia: "Powerful. For someone who's struggling with emotional turbulence, what's your first piece of advice?"

David: "Start by acknowledging your emotions. Journaling helps clarify thoughts and feelings. The act of writing brings insight and fosters awareness."

Mia: "Absolutely. Emotional regulation starts with awareness; it's a matter of honoring what we feel without being ruled by it. Every decision propels us toward healing."

As they continue, the listeners are reminded that each moment of emotional clarity grows into a path of personal growth and resilience.

The Power of Mindset: A Motivational Message

Mindset matters when discussing emotional regulation. Your emotional response is what makes or breaks reality. You go from feeling overwhelmed to empowered by changing the way you think and by adding stress management tools. Think about it. Each wave of emotion becomes an opportunity for growth. Your journey becomes a testament to your inner strength.

Therapeutic Approach & Healing Moment: A Guided Shift

Therapeutic Moment:

Take a moment to center yourself with a gentle breath. Close your eyes and recall a time when emotions clouded your judgment. Reflect on the thoughts accompanying that moment: were they rooted in fear, or were they guiding you? Release any weighty emotions and envision a new narrative filled with clarity and calmness. Instead of lingering in "I am stressed," embrace "I will navigate this." This shift cultivates peace and empowers your journey.

Final Thoughts: Capturing Your Inner Power

The things of which you are capable lie in taking control over your emotions and dealing with the stressful situations that you face. Every thought and every emotion is a part of a story you build day after day. By opening your doors to life with balance and grit, you learn to make the right choices by becoming more aware through the tools you choose. Understand that your emotions are not signs of struggle but instruments of growth to help you find yourself.

Reflection Prompt/Closing Thoughts:

As you progress with your emotional terrain, ask yourself:

- How are you actually listening to the emotions that arise for you in your everyday life?
- What are the subtle shifts in your emotional responses that lead to monumental shifts in your life experience?
- What would it look like to view every emotion as a teacher, inviting growth into your life?

Your path to emotional regulation leads to self-discovery and empowerment. Accept what you have, for it creates the reality in which you live.

6.3) The Significance of Psychotherapy and Professionals

Introduction: Packing the Layers of the Mind

Imagine, for a moment, walking through a world where each corner is a thought, a fear, or a buried memory. Among the nuances of our internal landscape lies the reality that healing often demands maps made by those experienced at navigating the therapists and professionals dedicated to guiding the way. What would it mean to find the argument for seeking therapy as a sign of power rather than weakness on the path to discovering the self? The mind is subtle and deep, full of beauty and chaos. Professional help can shed light on the journey, allowing us to walk in understanding with those we have been observing.

Quotes: Sparks of Insight

- *"The greatest discovery of my generation is that a human can alter his life by altering his attitude." —William James*

- *"The mind is like water. When it's agitated, it's hard to see; when it's calm, everything clears." —Prasad Mahesh*

These reflections evoke a sense of therapy's importance in bringing clarity to our minds that are wreaking havoc. They manifest the nature of change that awaits in our lives when we open ourselves to resources that are guided expertly, illustrating how learning can promote progress.

Poem: The Road to Recovery Through Therapy

"In the quiet of the mind, shadows creep.

Whispers of fears that we dare not keep.

But a guiding hand, still and wise,

May, through the shelter of its guise, be clear about what lies within.

There is a seed with every session in fertile ground,

Nourished by kindness, new truths are found.

With every shared thought, the burdens grow light;

We find our own light in the healing tapestry."

This poem encapsulates the tender relationship between seeker and guide, illustrating how therapy nurtures the mind and heart. It portrays the transformative power of conversation, encouraging exploration and healing.

Relatable Stories: Journeys of Healing

Let me tell the story of Liam, who lived with shadows of anxiety for so long. Every day was an uphill battle with no end in view. After encountering a therapist one day, he took the bold step into the domain of professional assistance. Liam told his therapist about how doubtful he felt about availing himself of such professional support. His therapist replied quietly, "Let us walk with the emotions. Most developments and even growth begin from vulnerability."

But in his sessions, he tore down the walls that he had constructed. He found that sharing himself was not a burden but freeing. The storms of worry began to temper, and a new depth of peace bloomed. His reality transformed; weight was lifted off, and hope unfurled like petals of flowers in spring. Strength began to surface in every act of his therapy journey, as opposed to merely pointing out what is wrong.

Exercises & Reflective Questions: Steps to Clarity

Exercise: Emotion Diary

Keep a diary of your emotions for the next week. Each day, record the emotions you experience. Pay more attention to the tougher ones. Consider reviewing this diary with a therapist to gain a better perspective.

Reflective Question:

What emotions are most likely to overwhelm you? How can you identify those feelings in a way that leads you toward the support you need?

Healing Moment:

Breathe and remember a time when you felt as though you faced your pain alone. What if you could invite someone into that space rather than pushing it away? Let this create a vision of healing and understanding.

Cinematic Approach: The Silver Screen Journey

Consider your life as a movie, where the protagonist stands amidst chaos, surrounded by churning doubts and fears. During such a time, it's as if you need help, and that person appears. Often, that person becomes your guiding light in the dark; he helps you clear away emotional rubble. There are moments of triumph over fears, unpacking the slow but profound process of trauma, and the path towards resilience. Credits roll as survival is not only achieved but flourishes, all thanks to the nurturing embrace of professional support.

Dialogue of Change: Panel Discussion

Navigating Therapy: Voices of Experience

Join the discussion of Mia, Jai, Leila, and Arjun as they share their observations on the importance of therapy in personal change.

Mia: "Today, we're talking about how therapy can truly change people's lives. Jai, do you think it's helpful to share yourself with someone who is professionally qualified?"

Jai: "Absolutely, Mia. I think therapy is a very safe platform where you can think, say, and basically feel your thoughts and whatever you have inside your heart without judgment. It's a deep opportunity for self-exploration."

Leila: "Exactly, Jai. When you start talking about your problems, you begin to process them. It's not just something to unburden; it's about knowing and gaining clarity."

Arjun: "Well, I can remember vividly when I first spoke about my experience. It was like turning on the light in a dark room. That simple act opened up healing pathways that I didn't even know existed."

Mia: "Wow, such great insights! For those fighting the stigmas attached to therapy, what truths would you share?"

Jai:"Therapy isn't a sign of failure; it's a tool for empowerment. It's a declaration that you are ready to embrace change."

Leila: "And it's okay to seek help. Everyone deserves support, just as we support others."

Conclusion: Finally, they urge the audience to see therapy not as the end but as a step in the process toward self-actualization.

The Power of Support: A Motivational Message

A universal truth stands before it all: professional support is the foundation of healing. Searching for help takes courage. As your mind opens to the expertise, you will no longer view life's challenges as insurmountable obstacles but as opportunities.

Change does not require a facelift on the outside, as it grows from within. It is through a professional that one recovers their life-legend story, showcasing how helpful therapy can be in rewriting your screenplay.

Therapeutic Approach & Healing Moment: A Facilitated Change

Therapeutic Moment:

Breathe in, and let your thoughts settle. Reflect on a time when you felt all thumbs. Think about what caught you in that mindset, and consider how some guidance might have helped you change that thinking. Imagine yourself unlocking the door to a therapeutic space where your feelings are heard and transformed into understanding. Feel the weight of burdens beginning to lift, bringing you a little bit closer with each moment to a place of clarity and strength.

Final Thought: Embrace Your Inner Strength

The act of seeking therapy is an empowering choice. It is an acknowledgment of the complexities of the human experience and a commitment to self-discovery. By becoming more mindful of your mental landscape and choosing to navigate it with professional support, you unveil endless possibilities for healing and personal growth.

Reflection Prompt/Closing Thoughts:

Consider the following questions while reflecting upon the importance of therapy in your life:

- How have you come to conceptualize seeking help over time?
- What emotions arise for you when you think of professional support?
- How might embracing the therapy journey impact your course toward healing?

Welcome the realization that your mind is an ocean of so much potential and with professional support, you can dive down into those depths and navigate toward that horizon of connection, healing, and hope.

Chapter 7: Embracing Spirituality and Mindfulness

Introduction:

Spirituality invites us in such moments of reflection to reach out to something greater; it gives clarity and meaning. Mindfulness helps people stay anchored in the present moment, fully experiencing life. Together, they pave the way to inner peace and purpose.

This chapter explores how spirituality fosters belonging, mindfulness leads to presence, and gratitude changes our view. Through stories, quotes, and exercises, you will find ways to incorporate these powerful tools into your life, deepening your connection to yourself and the world.

7.1) Defining Spirituality and Its Role in Personal Fulfillment

Introduction: The Essence of identity

Imagine stepping into the very core of your soul to find that connection that is beyond the. Spirituality is that profound journey, a time to look inward where the mysteries of existence bang into the core of who we are.

What if we understand that nurturing our spiritual self isn't a luxury but a necessity for complete fulfillment? Every individual has an interesting spiritual essence, one shaped by beliefs, experiences, and the intricate tapestry of life itself. Spirituality finds us in the threads that weave our existence together to identify our purpose and place in this world.

Quotes: Wisdom from the Ambassadors

- *"Spirituality does not come from religion. It comes from our soul." — Iyanla Vanzant*
- *"The only journey is the journey within." — Rainer Maria Rilke*
- *"Each of us is a miracle, and we all have a purpose. Seek from within the guidance you desire." — Oprah Winfrey*

These quotes are gentle reminders that spirituality makes up our personal compass and leads our ways, no matter how chaotic the outside world is. They unlock a universal truth: fulfillment and meaning are intertwined with our spiritual journey.

Poems: The Heart of Spiritual Growth

"Silence of the night so deep,

Awakens the soul, a yearning steep.

Every whisper of the heart's embrace,

Invites us to explore, to seek, to trace.

Spiritual rivers that flow within,

Feed the roots where our lives begin.

Nurtured by love and moments of grace,

Personal fulfillment, a sacred space."

This poem encapsulates the beat of spiritual exploration, expressing how each step in the stride of the spiritual path nourishes our quest for fulfillment, making it easier to connect with our innermost selves.

Relatable Stories: A Wake-Up Call to the Truth

For example, consider the story of Mark, an individual who invested a minimum of fifteen years in the struggle up the corporate ladder. He earned accolades and rose through the ranks, yet felt an unshakable hollow inside. One day, as he was passing by, he came upon a meditation group. "What if there's more to life than achievement?" they asked. Mark was skeptical yet fascinated, so he took his place among them. Time would tell what the solace of stillness and communion with kindred spirits on this different path would bring. Just as he was opening up his spiritual self, he began to realize that true satisfaction didn't stem from piling up accolades but from growing relationships, compassion, and understanding.

His world changed and reflected a depth of peace he had yearned for so long.

Exercises & Reflective Questions: Cultivating Your Spirituality

Exercise: Setting Daily Intentions

Each morning, take a minute to set an intention for that day. Something as simple as "I will seize joy in little moments" or "I will show compassion to myself and others." Notice how those small acts alter your experiences throughout the day.

Reflective Question:

Is there a particular time of day or a specific activity that makes you feel closest to your spiritual self?

Healing Moment:

Stop for a moment. Close your eyes and breathe deeply. Think of a time when you were spiritually alive. What kind of situation allowed that connection to thrive? Imagine rekindling that spark in your life today. How does this influence your sense of fulfillment?

Cinematic Method: Your Spiritual Journey as a Movie

Think of yourself as the protagonist of a personal development movie. The opening scene shows you living a life determined by the tick boxes on your societal checklist. Now, though, the plot twist arrives: you meet a sage mentor or accidentally stumble upon an old book that sparks something within you. That spark leads you through introspection, bringing you to your spiritual self. The scenes unfold through moments of doubt, joy, struggle, and revelation.

At every act of bravery and every connection made on the path, you begin to reveal the beautiful tapestry of your soul, culminating in a climactic scene of profound understanding and fulfillment.

Conversations of Change: A Podcast Dialogue

Reflections on Spirituality: Jenna's Insight

Join Jenna as she explores the meaning of spirituality in our lives.

"Today, I want to share a vital aspect of living fully: spirituality. It's not something bound by doctrine or dogma but a personal exploration. If we listen to that inner voice, we begin, in small but profound ways, to connect with the universe. Take my friend, Lila. For years, she felt lost and found herself searching. When she finally allowed herself to explore various spiritual practices, yoga, meditation, and mindfulness she started peeling off those layers that had been inhibiting her."

Its beauty lies in the fact that spirituality helps us cultivate a sense of belonging, personal serenity, and inner peace. Each practice is a stepping stone on a fragile bridge that leads to fulfillment. So, the question remains: What does spirituality evoke in you? How can it mold your journey toward individual satisfaction?

"Let's reflect on our individual practices and listen to the whispers of our souls. The profound realization is that our spirituality invites us to embody our true selves; each thought and action aligns with that authenticity."

The Power of Spiritual Mindset: A Motivational Message

Spirituality equips us to transcend the ordinary and tap into a fount of possibilities. It teaches us that satisfaction does not arise from the physical but from the depth of our understanding of ourselves. Changing our attitude toward being spiritual changes our perspective: every problem is an opportunity to learn, and every joy is a blessing. Through such a holistic view of life, we open ourselves to a life of purpose and connection.

Therapeutic Approach & Healing Moment: Assisted Change

Therapeutic Moment:

Deep breathing. Imagine a time when you felt disconnected or overwhelmed. Notice what thoughts were present at that time; were they perhaps fear-based or limiting? Consider the feelings you experienced, and even think of a renewal phrase to end this with: "What if I am enough just as I am?" This shift should make your heart feel more sensitive; you are reminded of the innately worthy aspects of yourself and your relationship with the universe.

Final Thought: The Stirring of Inner Wisdom

Beneath each of us resides a spring of spiritual wisdom, which awaits acknowledgment and nurturing. Attuning ourselves to our inner voice is the way to personal fulfillment, but it also opens the door for greater peace, joy, and understanding. Spirituality calls each of us to our true selves, to lead lives of profundity and purpose.

Reflection Prompt/Closing Thoughts

As you walk your spiritual path, consider how often you pause to ponder these questions:

- How connected are you to understanding your spiritual needs and desires?
- What subtle changes in practice might contribute to a sense of completion?
- Imagine walking daily with the lenses of spiritual discernment for whatever choice you make. What would that actually change in your world?

Your spirit is where your lifetime energies find their passage. Cultivate it and see how beautifully life falls into place.

7.2) Mindfulness Practices: Meditation, Breathing, and Presence

Introduction: The Art of Being Present

Imagine stepping into a moment everything fades away the noise, the distractions and all that's left is a sense of being. In cultivating mindfulness, we learn to ground ourselves in the present moment. Breath becomes an anchor, each thought an opportunity to explore the depths of our consciousness. What if today you could embrace the power of being fully in the present, with your mind and body aligned in perfect harmony? Mindfulness is more than a practice; it's an art to find oneself completely in each moment.

Quotes: Enlightening the Way to Mindfulness

- *"Mindfulness is a way of befriending ourselves and our experience." — Jon Kabat-Zinn*
- *"The greatest weapon against stress is our ability to choose one thought over another." — William James*
- *"Breath is the bridge which connects life to consciousness, which unites your body to your thoughts." — Thich Nhat Hanh*

These profound thoughts remind us that mindfulness is not a destination but a journey beginning with a single breath, guiding us back to ourselves.

Poem: The Essence of Mindfulness

"In the silence, the world unfolds,

A tapestry of moments, tales untold.

With every breath, serenity breathes,

In this space, the heart believes.

Thoughts like clouds, drifting by,

In stillness, the mind learns to fly.

Present and aware, the soul ignites,

Mindfulness whispers, "You are the light."

This poem encapsulates the delicate interplay between awareness and existence. As we allow ourselves to be present, we discover the beauty within each moment, a gift waiting to be unwrapped.

Stories We Can Identify With: A Shift in Awareness

Take the case of Leo, a high-powered professional caught up in the whirlwind of his work. The deadlines and meetings had reduced him to mere spectatorship in his own life. It was only after an accidental encounter with one of his old friends, who was a mindfulness practitioner, that Leo started noticing the beauty in things.

"Try meditating for just five minutes each day," his friend suggested. Skeptical but curious, Leo embarked on this small venture. The first several attempts strained at his very mind, his thoughts flying about things he had to do and obligations. Gradually, however, the practice began to blossom; he began to delight in the peace of the present moment. Leo became much more present at work, more present in conversations, and eventually much more at peace with his life. Such slight movement in consciousness changed his world, filling his days with purpose and purposefulness.

Exercises & Reflective Questions: Developing Mindfulness

Exercise: Breathing into Stillness

Take five minutes each day. Sit comfortably. Close your eyes and breathe in slowly through your nostrils. Let your abdomen rise as you fill your lungs with air. Pause for a second, and then exhale very slowly through your mouth. Feel the sensation of the air entering and leaving your body as you breathe. If your mind begins to wander, gently return it to your breath.

Reflective Question:

What happens in your body when you take a few moments to breathe more slowly and deeply? How do you observe shifts in your emotional landscape as you focus your attention on your breath?

Healing Moment:

Take a minute of silence. Breathe three deep breaths, in calmness and out tension. Remember the time when breathing eased your confusion. What was it like? Picture an entire mess of entanglements calming with every breath being steady, here, and peaceful.

Cinematic Perspective: Your Life on the Screen of the Now

Imagine your life is a movie unfolding on the screen of now. Each scene holds the weight of your thoughts, emotions, and reactions. The camera panning from one moment to another grips you with anxiety over what's next or regret for something in the past. A new figure must step in a wise one, a mentor, whispering about the importance of presence. Then, the story changes as you learn how to anchor in the present. The story develops into a character whose living of every moment builds to insightful revelations and healing. The final scene can be seen as a life of mindfulness that is, one has journeyed from awareness.

Conversations of Change: A Podcast Dialogue

Mindful Moments with Alex: A Journey into Presence

Take the deep conversation about mindfulness with Alex.

Alex: "Today's topic relates to one that has struck each of us so deeply: the practice of mindfulness. It is rather astonishing to ponder how, swept away by the currents of life, we forget this beautiful feeling of 'being' in its purest form."

"I would love to share a story about one student whom I used to see a lot. This was Maya. She felt overwhelmed by multiple responsibilities and constantly found herself multitasking. During one workshop, while practicing mindful breathing, Maya was surprised by how even short moments of presence could shift her frenetic energy, completely altering her perspective. She began to incorporate brief moments of mindfulness into her daily routine in line for meals, while commuting breathing and reconnecting with herself.

"The change is profound. When we commit to simply being, we clear out the clutter and let joy flow in to resuscitate our experiences.

"Do you feel you are ready to show up to each present moment with intention and love? Today's podcast invites you to consider how mindfulness might manifest in your reality and what your journey looks like in the comments."

The Power of Mindfulness: A Message in Motivation

Mindfulness reveals a universal truth: in stillness, there is power. The way you engage with each moment creates waves that extend far beyond your own personal experience. The lovely thing about mindfulness is that it doesn't need to be perfect, it invites presence. As you become more aware of the whispers of thoughts and emotions, you now have the opportunity to respond instead of react, an important element in crafting a life of intention and joy.

Therapeutic Approach & Healing Moment: Facilitating Change

Therapeutic Moment:

Take a deep breath in. Close your eyes and remember a moment in which you were overwhelmed or disconnected. Notice the thoughts that were knocking about your mind at the time. Consciously let go of any negativity you find yourself entombed with in that thought. Now breathe in a more positive mindset, changing "I cannot find peace" into "I open myself up to peace and the now." Repeat this to yourself, and let the change resound as you dive into greater self-knowledge.

Final Insight: Gateway to the Mind's Presence

The secret of mindfulness is actually inwardly within; the fact that a moment is full of peace, joy, and fulfillment. Nurturing and cultivating the practice of being present can mold your reality to choose being actively involved with life rather than passively living it. Every moment becomes an invitation to connect, breathe, and be truly alive.

Reflective Prompt/Closing Thoughts:

As you go about your path of developing mindfulness, consider for a moment:

- How often do you get swept up in your thoughts and miss what the present has to offer?
- What is one small mindfulness practice that you could commit to cultivating in your life?

- What would shift if you were to take presence fully to heart?

Your path to mindfulness awaits you. Devote it consciously and see how all aspects of your life emerge in clear, distinct truthfulness.

7.3) Inspiring Gratitude and Its Magic of Transmutation

Introduction: The Alchemy of Appreciation

Imagine a life with gratitude seeping into every moment, transmuting the banal into the extraordinary. What if one could command gratitude's power to mold experiences, even in the dark corners of the mind? Being grateful is not just a fleeting feeling but an alchemical power that can uplift your life toward greater emotional balance and intimacy with the environment. As you develop conscious gratitude, you build an inner sanctuary full of joy and appreciation, allowing you to navigate life with a new perspective.

Quotes: Echoes of Enlightenment

- *"Gratitude is not only the greatest of virtues but the parent of all the others." — Marcus Tullius Cicero*

- *"Gratitude turns what we have into enough." — Melody Beattie*
- *"Reflect upon your present blessings, of which every man has plenty; not on your past misfortunes, of which all men have some." — Charles Dickens*

These proverbs remind us that a grateful attitude is a propelling force moving us toward greater fulfillment. In addition, they unravel the mystery of realizing that what we appreciate opens up a life full of abundance.

Poem: The Language of the Heart

"In stillness, gratitude takes root,

A soft-brimmed seed of kindness glows.

Nurture it each day; let it grow,

A tapestry woven by a loving hand.

Grateful hearts sing and dance;

In the light of abundance, we find our stance.

What we love, we begin to see;

The world unfolds in sweet harmony."

This is a poem of gratitude and infinite possibility, filled with appreciation, cultivating experiences that create the mosaic of our reality, painting it in colors of hope, joy, and love.

Stories to Relate: Awakening the Heart

Consider the story of Samuel, whose burden was discontent. Every day became a fight, and most of the time, he would talk about what was missing in life: financial security, fulfilling relationships, and purpose. At a friend's insistence, one day Samuel agreed to maintain a gratitude journal. Incredulous yet curious, Samuel agreed to write down three things for which he was thankful each day.

As the week progressed, Samuel found that something was moving beneath the surface. He began looking at life from a different perspective. Even the small things, the warmth of the sun on his skin, the laughter he shared with friends, the mouthwatering taste of a home-cooked meal ignited a spark within him to live with joy again. What had once weighed heavily on his heart with discontent now seemed lighter, and he began to see life differently. He learned that gratitude is not about circumstances but a decision to find beauty in the ordinary things and people around us.

Exercises & Reflective Questions: Cultivating an Attitude of Gratitude

Exercise: Gratitude Reflection

Dedicate a few minutes each evening to reflect on the day. Write down three moments of gratitude. They can be as small as a warm cup of tea or as significant as a heartfelt conversation. Over time, notice how this practice shifts your perspective.

Reflective Questions:

When faced with challenges, do you default to negative thoughts? How might a focus on gratitude alter your experience at that moment?

Healing Moment:

Pause and breathe deeply. Recall an experience from today that brought you a sense of gratitude. As you inhale, draw in the warmth of that feeling; let it bring you more peace. Let this experience remind you of the abundance that already surrounds your life.

Film Approach: Your Gratitude Movie

Consider that you are the leading star of an inspiring film. The opening scene reveals you wandering through a confusing world, shrouded by cloudy negativity. You then find a mentor who teaches you about gratitude, and the story begins when you start documenting your daily blessings and discovering the extraordinary in the ordinary. During this evolution, the camera captures your inner change; connections deepen, joy amplifies, and you awaken to the magic of life. The final scene shows you glowing, fully immersed in appreciation, living life with purpose and connection.

Change Conversations: A Gratitude Dialogue Ending Scene

The Transformative Journey of Gratitude: A Chat between Mia and Leo

Leo: "Mia, I have noticed something in you lately. What's going on?"

Mia: "It's gratitude, Leo. Keeping a gratitude journal has made a real difference for me. It's no longer about what I am missing out on but about the depth of my experiences."

Leo: "That's interesting. So, how did you first apply that in your life?"

Mia: "Well, I began very small, just writing down three things at the end of each day. It felt almost like a chore when I first started, but soon, I began looking forward to those moments of gratitude throughout the day!"

Leo: "That's powerful. So now, gratitude has become a lens through which you view life?"

Mia: "Exactly! It's not just a list; it's a mindset. You know, like watering a garden? You see the growth only if you nurture it."

Leo: "Wow, such insight. What would you suggest for someone who feels stuck in negativity?"

Mia: "Start small. Choose one moment of gratitude each day and watch how that seed grows. Before you know it, the light will be pouring in."

The Power of Mindset: A Gratitude-Driven Perspective

Understand this basic truth: gratitude is transformative. It shapes the very foundation of your mindset, opening avenues previously shrouded in doubt and hopelessness. With every conscious choice toward gratitude, you shift from viewing a situation as a barrier to seeing it as an opportunity. The process of becoming grateful allows you to discover the goodness in life and shifts your perspective from scarcity to abundance.

Therapeutic Approach & Healing Moment: A Guided Changeover

Therapeutic Moment:

Deepen your breath and ground yourself. Think of a moment when you were overwhelmed by unhappiness. Witness that moment and observe what was going through your mind without judgment. Next, replace those thoughts with thanksgiving: "What did I learn? What strength did I gain?" Allow this healing shift to resonate within you. You possess the ability to redefine your personal history with gratitude.

Final Thought: Embracing Your Inner Light

Gratitude is a powerful catalyst that can open your eyes to the potential of living a life of joy and fulfillment. Every thought of appreciation you plant grows the fabric of your reality and allows you to become more connected and fulfilled in all that you do. Through the integration of gratitude into your life, you unlock the door to possibility, and your life begins to unfurl with the beauty that lies within.

Reflection Prompt/Closing Thoughts:

Beginning this journey of gratitude means taking a little time to reflect on the following:

- How often do you consciously express gratitude in your everyday life?
- What is one tiny act of gratitude that you will integrate into your routine this week?
- How would your life change if, from day to day, you viewed it through the eyes of appreciation?

It is only within you that your ability to fulfill lies. Nurture a heart of thanks and start to envision a reality that unfolds from your most intimate thoughts, desires, and aspirations.

Chapter 8: Discovering Life Purpose and Personal Fulfillment

Introduction:

Life is all too often an exploration for the meaning that goes beyond all words. Most of us can't explain what fully satisfies them. In this chapter, we are going to look at how you could discover your purpose in life through passion and values, because only then can one find his actions truly thrilling, authentic, and filled with meaning. Join me as I try to guide you on this path for an intentional fulfillment of one's life.

8.1) Strategies for Uncovering Personal Passion and Meaning

Introduction: Unlocking Your Inner Compass

Imagine standing at a crossroads. Each path speaks with a sound of potential personal fulfillment and meaning. If you learn that the compass guiding your way is fashioned from the passions hidden deep within your being, then a flicker of excitement creates a mosaic of your purpose. By discovering those natural desires, you may illuminate your pathway to a life full of authenticity and laughter. Knowing what makes your soul on fire is not just a journey; it's an awakening that transforms the way you experience the mundane.

Quotes: Wisdom that Guides

- *"The only way to do great work is to love what you do." — Steve Jobs*
- *"Your time is limited; don't waste it living someone else's life." — Steve Jobs*
- *"Find ecstasy in life; the mere sense of living is joy enough." — Emily Dickinson*

These profound words echo the sentiment that our passions are integral to our existence. They remind us to seek out the activities and pursuits that resonate with our true selves, illuminating our personal paths.

Poem: Spirit of Passion

"Whispers of joy tenderly begin,

Within the shadows of your heart.

Follow them wherever they may lead;

In passion's light, your soul's freed.

Like twinkling stars on nights so bright,

Your passions shine like radiant light.

Embrace them and let them grow;

Within them lie stories yet untold."

This poetic reflection captures the pursuit of passion; for when we listen to the inner whispers of joy, we step into a narrative that is uniquely ours.

Relatable Stories: A Journey of Discovery

Take the case of James, a man still trapped in the web of society's expectations. For years, James worked off a prescribed track: good titles, good paychecks, while suppressing the quiet yearning for creativity that nudged from within him. One fateful evening, he chanced upon a community art class and signed up with both trepidation and excitement.

The moment his brush kissed the paint, he began to transform. Colors started flowing onto the canvas; years of untold joy and passion bottled up inside him suddenly began overflowing. That one decision unraveled into a cascade of others: new friendships, exhibitions, and ultimately, clarity on what he was meant to do in life. In embracing his passion, James shifted the narrative of his life to align with who he was supposed to be.

Exercises & Reflective Questions: Discover Your Passions

Exercise: Passion Inventory

Identify some things that excite you. Remember when you really felt like you were living. What were you doing at the time? What feelings did you have? This inventory will prove to be a great discovery of your real interests.

Reflective Questions:

What are some things that you can do that just capture your attention and make time melt away? How can you incorporate more of those things into your life?

Healing Moment:

Sit quietly, imagining a day of activities that align with your passion. How do you feel? Let that vision brew inside. Note what hesitations come up and how you can respectfully work through those barriers to engage with your passion.

Cinematic Approach: Your Life as a Movie

Imagine that life is a big film. It starts with you going through a pretty ordinary routine in the first few scenes. Suddenly, though, it gets exciting maybe due to a surprise encounter or a new opportunity. The music builds into a crescendo as you embark on an adventure of self-discovery, trying hobbies, interests, and aspirations you used to save for when you had time. This is when the climax bursts, as you fully embrace your passions, leading to a compelling transformation that captivates not only you but everyone around you. As the credits roll, you stand tall as the vibrant protagonist, one who has unearthed a purpose, creating a meaningful story.

Conversations of Change: A Podcast Dialogue

Finding Your Passion: A Dialogue with Maria and David

Let's listen to Maria and David as they delve into the art of discovering personal passion:

Maria: "David, when we engage with our passions, it feels like a journey of courage and exploration. What was that pivotal moment for you?"

David: "It hit me during a totally unexciting work meeting. I realized that concepts that had once thrilled me were just whispers in a cacophony of noise. It ignited a search to reestablish those passions."

Maria: "That is so interesting! I sometimes think about how fear can be a silencer. What did you do to break through that?"

David: "By starting small. I took a weekend pottery class. Each finished piece became a reminder that even tiny steps can illuminate forgotten paths. It was a leap toward my purpose."

Maria: "What advice would you give someone unsure of where to start?"

David: "Start with curiosity. Experiment, explore, and let the sparks you feel guide you. It's not just about finding one thing but realizing you can cultivate many."

As their conversation unfolds, mutual encouragement surrounds the listeners, urging everyone to walk this path of discovery to find what will truly set them ablaze.

The Inspirational Message in Mindset

Understand that discovering your passions is actually an inside job. By being curious and open to life, you allow for discovery and growth. Everything that happens in your life, leading you toward or away from your passions, is a lesson. Confronting challenges, rather than avoiding them, clarifies and strengthens the journey toward purpose.

Therapeutic Approach & Healing Moment: A Guided Shift

Therapeutic Moment:

Take a deep breath in and allow the breath to fill your being. Imagine a moment in time when your heart leapt at the prospect of pursuing a dream. Now, think about what limiting beliefs arose as you contemplated this pursuit. See yourself lightly letting go of those thoughts and embracing this idea instead: "What if I pursue my passion?" Let that yearning for space ignite an extraordinary flame of possibility within.

Conclusion: Your Journey Begins Within

At the end of everything, your journey of self-discovery is full of introspection and self-exploration. Try to become more sensitive to the desires bubbling inside you as you go through life. Your passions are not hobbies; they are integral strings woven into the tapestry of your purpose. Learn to love them, nurture them, and allow them to transform your reality.

Reflective Question/Closing Lines:

As you embark on this journey of discovery, take time to reflect on the following:

- What has always brought passion to your life? Do you currently experience those passions in your life?
- How might spending time on new passions redefine what's possible?
- Imagine living a life filled with passion and purpose. How might that resonate within you?

It is in pursuing passions that one finds his voice and purpose the essence of who he is. The wait is over; start your journey today.

8.2) Aligned Actions with Core Values and Goals

Introduction: Your Compass

Consider taking steps in a journey, guided by the compass signifying your values and goals. This compass is not one to be discovered in some distant land but rather lives inside you. What if today you decide to align your actions with the essence of who you are? It is a time to choose between anchoring in your values and getting diverted into the abyss of distractions, confusion, and noise every decision, every routine, and every passing moment. Your core values are your north star, illuminating the path toward a life abounding with purpose and authenticity.

Quotes: Catalysts for Reflection

- *"Values are not just a piece of paper you hang on your wall; they're the ground level beneath which meaningful actions are created." — Anonymous*
- *"Your values are your GPS. They guide you to where you want to go, or they keep you in a place you don't want to be." — Anonymous*
- *"The things you own end up owning you. It's only after you lose everything that you're free to do anything." — Chuck Palahniuk*

Each of these quotes reminds us, at the right time, that living our daily lives according to our values allows us to see things for what they are in the midst of such a distracting world. They show how self-awareness shapes a life that is meant to be lived with purpose and intent.

Poems: The Dance of Actions and Values

"A kite of values, steady and bright,

In every act, they settle and take flight.

With every step, let purpose resound,

For in harmony of motion, joy is found.

When values guide each choice we make,

A tapestry of sense we weave and break.

In the glass of our lives, we may see,

The vision of our truth, vibrant and free."

In this poem, a relationship is described in harmonious accord between our actions and the virtues closest to our hearts. It vividly illustrates how conscious alignment can transform mundane tasks into meaningful, empowering experiences.

Relatable Stories: The Journey of Alignment

Take Alex, a dedicated professional who constantly felt overwhelmed by the demands of his job. For years, he chased success as defined by societal standards: long hours, impressive titles, and an overflowing email inbox. Yet, there was a growing feeling of discontent driving home in the background, saying that something essential was missing.

One evening, after a really exhausting day, Alex was lucky enough to tune into a conversation about values. A close friend was talking about the journey of rediscovery: "When I realized that my actions were not aligned with my core values, such as family, health, and creativity, I felt like I was just running in circles." It struck a chord with Alex.

He wrote down his core values: family, growth, and balance. Immediately, Alex began to make small adjustments to things like setting boundaries at work, dedicating evenings to the loved ones he had neglected for so long, and really pursuing his hobby of painting. Slowly, a shift occurred. The frustration started to melt away, replaced by renewed peace and fulfillment. Every day now had purpose, and his life started reflecting what mattered most.

Exercises & Reflective Questions: Walking the Way

Exercise: Core Values Exercise

Take a day to reflect on your core. Write down the values that feel most alive for you. For each value, provide one action you will take this week to live in congruence with it.

Reflective Questions:

What are some daily actions that are currently out of alignment with core values? How might you shift just one action week to live in greater alignment?

Healing Moment:

Close your eyes and imagine a day where every action connects with your core values. Feel the power of living authentically. What happens to your emotions and experiences when you can bring your life more fully in line with what matters most?

Cinematic Approach: Directing Your Life's Story

Picture this: you are the director of a strong story. In the beginning scene, you are caught in a whirlwind of conflicting responsibilities and pressures. As the plot unfolds, you come across a turning point, a moment where there is a realization that shifts the narrative. Maybe it is a conversation, a troubled situation, or even a lonely moment where you remember what really matters to you.

As the story unfolds, you start weaving deliberate scenes that underline your core values onto the screen. Every chosen value affects the choices made along the way, giving rise to meaningful relationships and richer experiences. In the final act, you are portraying a character who has been transformed not by the absence of challenges but through strength in alignment with themselves.

Conversations of Change: A Podcast Dialogue

Values Reflections by Emma Insightful Journey

Let's tune in to a private conversation with Emma as she digs deeper into the profound connection between everyday actions and core values.

Emma: "What we are doing is not a reflection of what we support and stand behind. Sometimes in life, how many things do we lose ourselves from that really matter? For instance, I have been through situations where everything around you did not seem to connect to your sense of purpose. Then a mentor sat me down and asked, 'What do you stand for? What connects with your heart?'

"This simple question led me down a path of clarity. I began seeing that my values, really my morals, have been important in guiding my life. The little things I've done, like making time for family dinner or creating some space for creative time, anchored me back to those values."

So, here's a thought provoking question for you: Are you the hero of your own life story or just a side character? Every one of your actions is an opportunity to make your values visible. Progress, not perfection that's what encourages me to go back in the light of the day, sort out your daily choices, and pick one that's aligned with the true nature of who you are.

Emma concludes by asking the listener to take the choices they make as statements of their values so that every little step toward alignment makes the story of their lives richer.

The Power of Mindset: A Motivational Message

It is here, at the heart of all this, that lies a universal truth: values not only guide our actions but also shape our identities. Being intentional about aligning the daily activities of life with core values opens the tap of motivation and clarity, which fills a journey full of meaning. Life no longer becomes arbitrary; rather, it's empowered choices that make up a tapestry of fulfillment and purpose.

Remember that the process of transformation doesn't have to come through grand leaps; it starts with small, intentional steps into alignment. You give yourself the power to revise the story of your life when you acknowledge how your values are shaping you.

Therapeutic Approach & Healing Moment: A Guided Reflection

Therapeutic Moment:

Take a breath. Shut your eyes and remember a recent where your behavior was out of sync with your core values. Reflect on the feelings that arose during that time. Were they feelings of frustration, confusion, or longing? Gently acknowledge those emotions and let them go. Imagine a more empowering story: what would have happened if you were in alignment with your core values? Breathe in a sense of peace as you envision the strength that comes from living from your center.

Final Thought: Your Inner Power

The power to align your daily activities with the core values you possess lies within you. Each choice takes you closer to your authentic self or keeps you cycling in disconnection. As you work with mindfulness around your values and deliberately change your actions, you begin to open up a whole world of possibilities. Remember that your daily activities are building blocks to create a life that reflects your true essence, not just another task to be undertaken.

Closing Thoughts/Reflection Prompt:

Reflect for a moment on the path ahead of you.

- On a daily basis, how mindful are you of what you are doing as it relates to your core values?
- What small shift in action can create a ripple effect of transformation for your reality?
- What would it feel like to live your life from a place of alignment and integrity with your values each and every day?

Your values are the anchor. By cultivating them with conscious action, you begin to create a life that truly resonates with your truest self.

8.3) Purpose in Overall Well-being and Resilience

Introduction: Finding the Meaning of Purpose

Imagine a life richly interwoven with purpose, a tapestry made from lives, passions, and goals. Suppose it were possible to wake up one day with a sense direction that you knew wasn't just an idea, but part of yourself? Purpose goes beyond mere goals, creating the flame from within that will shape the writing of your story. Every action you take and every decision you make speaks to the fundamental importance of purpose in your life. It provides clarity during chaos and strength in the face of adversity, guiding you unyieldingly along your path.

Quote: Wisdom that Resonates

- *"Those who have a reason to live can bear almost any how."* — *Friedrich Nietzsche*
- *"Your purpose in life is to find your purpose and give your whole heart and soul to it."* — *Buddha*
- *"The greatest tragedy in life is not death, but a life without purpose."* — *Myles Munroe*

The words shed light on the apparent relationship between purpose and well-being. They remind us that a life of meaning is not just to be lived, but to be felt, loved, and strived for. Our purpose can guide us through the complexities of life.

Poem: A Journey in Purpose

"In the dead of night, flickering gleam

Shines bright; by heart it is aligned.

Purpose, our beacon, guiding star,

We venture forth, however far.

With each step, our spirits soar,

An anchored heart will seek more.

Resilience blooms where purpose grows.

In trials faced, together we choose."

This poem communicates the soul's deeply significant connection to purpose: how it feeds resilience and fuels well-being. Given that we adhere to our purpose, barriers become stepping stones that lead us toward wisdom and strength.

Shared Experience: The Source of Guidance

Take, for instance, Marcus, who used to be that aimless wanderer in life, lost amidst the din of expectations. Every day felt like a burden to overcome; a set of tasks devoid of joy and passion filled each day. Everything changed when a mentor introduced him to the concept of purpose. "What gives your life meaning, Marcus?" they asked, sparking something deep within him.He discovered what interested him in teaching through reflection and searching, and when he began sharing his knowledge, the fog of monotony lifted into a satisfying kind of fulfillment. The tests he once thought of as 'mistakes' become lessons in resilience through adversity.Life's path, once wandering, became vibrant with purpose.

Exercises & Reflective Questions: Developing Awareness

Exercise: Discovery Journal: Finding Purpose

Reflect on activities that bring excitement or happiness each day. Record moments that helped you come alive. Analyze the patterns and insights over the course of a week to determine the essence of your purpose.

Reflective Questions:

Which activities allow you to "lose track" of time? How might these moments reveal your sense of purpose?

Healing Moment:

Inhale, close your eyes, and remember the time that made you feel connected to your purpose. How would that change your emotions and relationships? Activate those feelings and let them guide you into a clearer vision of purpose now.

Cinematic Approach: Life as a Story

Imagine for a moment that you are the hero in an extremely compelling story. You're standing at a crossroads, with uncertainty carved across your face. A wise mentor comes before you, urging you to embark on a journey of discovering your purpose. The camera captures moments of doubt and clarity, frustration and inspiration, during trials and triumphs.The climax reveals your purpose intertwined with the lessons learned along the way. You emerge resilient not just surviving but truly thriving as the story unfolds. The final scene encapsulates a life rich with intention, where every chapter contributes to a larger narrative of fulfillment.

Conversations of Change: Podcast Insights

Reflecting on Resilience: Jamie's Perspective

Join Jamie as she answers her question about purpose while on a journey of discovering how that purpose fuels resilience.

"Today, let's explore how our purpose shapes our experiences. I've witnessed so many people transform their lives by identifying what truly matters to them. For instance, my friend Tara had always dreamt of conservation. Once she aligned her daily actions with that purpose, she found strength in adversity that was pivotal to her journey.""I recall a moment when Tara was overwhelmed with challenges. Rather than giving in to despair, she recalled her purpose and tapped into a source of resilience within herself. That connection between purpose and well-being is really what makes all the difference. Every action that aligns with our purpose builds up our ability to be resilient."

"Ask yourself, 'What drives my actions? What gives my life meaning?' By embracing these questions, you anchor yourself to a more resilient path."

The Sense of Purpose: A Call to Action

Purpose will form the basis upon which a fulfilling life is built. It influences our being, guiding us through triumph and trial. With a viewpoint toward purpose, every setback becomes an opportunity for growth, and every challenge becomes a pathway for learning. Transformation starts from the inside; by identifying and tapping into your purpose, you build the strength to face adversities in life.

Therapeutic Approach & Healing Moment: Guided Visualization

Therapeutic Moment:

Take a deep breath in. Close your eyes and reflect on a meaningful moment when you felt very clear about your direction. What thoughts and emotions accompanied this moment? Now think of something you're struggling with now. Shift your focus to how becoming the owner of your purpose can change your perspective. Rather than feeling powerless, envision reframing your thoughts as follows:

"How might my purpose help me get through this?" Let this image in your mind settle you in power and clarity.

Final Reflection: Your Path to Purpose

All that you do and every choice you make is on behalf of a purpose not a destination, but a force within. You lighten the way for resilience and well-being by growing in this awareness. Your thoughts and intentions take life; to actively cultivate them is to build a way forward one full of possibility and fulfillment.

Reflection Prompt/Closing Thoughts:

As you continue down your path, take a moment to reflect on:

- How often are you really accessing your sense of purpose each and every day?
- What's something small you can do today to start living more in alignment with that purpose?
- Imagine waking up each morning to the roar of the purpose engine. How might things change?

Embrace your purpose and watch how it transforms reality, creating resilience and adding to general well-being. The journey is yours to create.

Chapter 9: Committing to Continuous Growth and Improvement

Introduction:

Growth in life is a journey, not a destination. In this chapter, you will discover how to transform challenges into opportunities for self-improvement through adopting a growth mindset. When you believe that your abilities and intelligence are not fixed but may change, you open the door to being able to overcome obstacles and rise to new heights. In this section, you will discover how realistic goal setting and personal development lead to continuous improvement. You are getting closer to your best self with each step in the right mindset and a focus on progression.

9.1) The Concept of a Growth Mindset and Its Importance

Introduction: Shaping the World Within, Embracing Growth

A reality in which every setback is not a wall but a stepping stone; it's an opportunity for personal evolution. Imagine if you could see that the tougher times facing you are not barriers but priceless lessons in shaping your character; with this growth mindset comes a change in the fabric of your experiences to thrive in environments demanding resilience and adaptability. Every moment of struggle is an opportunity for growth and for gaining strength and wisdom, for shaping your journey through life.

Quotes: Words that Enlighten

- *"What we fear doing most is usually what we most need to do." — Tim Ferriss*
- *"Intelligence is not fixed; it can be developed." — Carol S. Dweck*
- *"Success is not the key to happiness. Happiness is the key to success. If you love what you are doing, you will be successful." — Albert Schweitzer*

These profound insights remind us that our mindset is not a static trait but a dynamic framework that can be cultivated. They illuminate the right path to understanding how accepting challenges leads us to growth and fulfillment.

Poem: The Dance of Possibility

"In every stumble, a lesson waits.

Within each challenge, skill creates.

Hatred of limits, love for the climb,

In the dance of growth, we find our rhyme.

Every step we take is a choice to expand,

With every struggle, a stronger stand.

The limits we break, heights reached and scaled,

In the spirit of growth, our fears transcend."

This poem captures the heart of the growth mindset, illustrating how challenges function as catalysts for development. It communicates that when we embrace such trials, we grow in resilience and bring out our best.

Great People Stories: Changed Perspectives

Take the case of Alex, for instance, whose life seemed more like a treadmill you run but never seem to get moving forward. Trapped in the most mundane job, he started posing profound questions to himself. One day, one of his colleagues said, "Growth happens when you get uncomfortable." This simple idea inspired a change within Alex. He opted to see each work task not as something he had to do but rather as something he could grow through.

The ordinary tasks became a way of learning and gaining self-esteem. Good conversations bloomed along with networking opportunities. His reality changed; Alex was no longer stagnant but instead emerged in a marvelous realm of possibilities.

Exercises & Reflective Questions: Cultivating a Growth Mindset

Exercise: Challenge Journal

Keep a challenge journal for two weeks. Every time an obstacle comes your way, write down your thoughts and feelings regarding this obstacle. Consciously replace negative interpretations with more empowering thoughts that promote a growth mindset. Conclude after two weeks and reflect on the changes you noticed in your mindset.

Reflective Questions:

When faced with a challenge, do you view it as a threat or a chance to learn? In what ways can this perspective influence your response?

Healing Moment:

Shut your eyes and breathe deeply in through your nose and out through your mouth. Think of a time when you saw failure as a disappointment rather than as a challenge. Now, imagine what that scenario might have looked like had you used a growth mindset there. Notice how it changes the emotional landscape of the situation.

Cinematic Method: Your Life is a Movie

Imagine yourself as the main character of your great story. In the opening sequence, you fight against self-doubt and limiting beliefs, blinded by the fear of failure. The story takes a pivotal turn with a mentor or a book, changing the way you understand growth. Suddenly, obstacles emerge not as villains but as integral plot points in your journey. The camera captures your evolution each setback, each lesson showing how you grow stronger and wiser. You win and celebrate your victories, but not only the ones of accomplishment but also those of bravery in tackling challenges.

Conversations of Change: Podcast Dialogue

The Growth Mindset: Shaping Your Path

Join an inspiring podcast dialogue with Sarah, Marco, Isabel, and Jason as they reflect on the transformative power of a growth mindset.

Sarah: "Today, we're going into the growth mindset, a cornerstone change for anyone seeking to develop. Marco, why do you think this is so important?"

Marco: "I believe it's just about our perception. When we see challenges as learning opportunities, we automatically become better at adapting and thriving."

Isabel: "Absolutely! Our minds are like gardens; we feed them with the belief that growth is possible, and we cultivate resilience and innovation."

Jason: "I hated my mistakes so much that embracing them as any form of experience opened me to so many doors. Now I see every difficulty as a thrilling adventure."

Sarah: "It's amazing how a mindset shift changes everything. If someone is scared of failure, how would you practically advise that person?"

Marco: "Take the first step. Frame failures as experiments and call them valuable learning experiences instead of defeat."

Isabel: "And surround yourself with people who inspire growth. Community can be the biggest motivator of all."

Jason: "Finally, don't hurry the process. It takes time for a growth mindset to find its way into your psyche. So be patient with yourself as you walk this journey."

They end by saying this: developing a growth mindset adjusts your inner dialogue in a way that illuminates the path to things once thought impossible.

Mindset: A Message for Motivation

One plain fact is that your mindset calls your shots in defining your story. Rewrite life's script with turnaround obstacles as the chances to grow so each one of those moments won't be a hurdle but rather one to pass on your way toward progress. You will acquire the power to move meaningfully and clearly through your world once you realize that you can own a growth mindset. Change begins from within; it is the solstice of self-awareness.

Therapeutic Approach & Healing Moment: A Guided Shift

Therapeutic Moment:

Take a deep breath. Close your eyes and return to a time when you experienced something that seemed to move backward. Bring the thoughts you had at the time forward. Were those thoughts more or less anchoring you in fear? Let those thoughts go now. Imagine an alternative story. Instead of "I can't," begin to ask yourself, "What if I can?" Embrace this shift, allowing it to bring strength and comfort.

Your thoughts hold immeasurable power in shaping not just your emotions but your entire reality.

Final Thought: Your Inner Power

The power to ignite change lives within you. Each thought you think either keeps you in your comfort zone or thrusts you into a realm of possibility. You unlock doors for new experiences that reflect your potential once you become intentional about embracing a growth mindset.

Reflection Prompt/Closing Thoughts:

Reflect on the following as you embark on this journey:

- How often do you encounter opportunities for growth in challenges?
- What change in mindset would be subtly revolutionary?
- Imagine you got up each morning with the thinking that fed on possibility, empowering you and what possibilities awaited you?

Your mind is the spark of everything you seek. With supportive, growth-oriented thinking, you begin to construct a reality that resonates with your highest aspirations.

9.2) Setting Realistic Goals for Ongoing Self-Improvement

Introduction: The Journey of Growth

Imagine standing at the crossroads of your life, where each path is an opportunity for growth and self-improvement. The goals you set act as guiding stars, illuminating the way forward. What if you embraced the mindset that every goal, whether grand or modest, is a stepping stone in your journey? Letting go of the supercritical expectation of making realistic goals changes your approach as well as the overall experience of life. In other words, goals that align with our true desires are the blueprint for our potential.

Quotes: Inspiration that Guides

- *"Success is the sum of small efforts, repeated day in and day out."* — Robert Collier
- *"Setting goals is the first step in turning the invisible into the visible."* — Tony Robbins
- *"The future belongs to those who believe in the beauty of their dreams."* — Eleanor Roosevelt

These sayings remind us that our dreams, if we set them in our minds properly, can become reality. They drive home such a simple yet profound truth: that even the most unattainable dreams can be realized through the gradual steps taken toward achieving them.

Poem: The Rhythm of Goals

In the soil of dreams, plant each seed.With patience and care, they'll grow indeed.Map your desires, take mindful strides,For every small goal, a treasure resides.

Each milestone reached is a song of grace,A testament to the journey you embrace.Through ups and downs, like waves on the shore,With real ambitions, you open all doors.

This poem breathes meaning and definition into goal-setting, wherein every realistic goal we set encourages us to seek more.

Relatable Stories: The Power of Realism

Consider a story about Michael, an eager fellow born to change. He first aimed too high; his lofty aims and wild aspirations were mountains rather than achievable objectives. He dreamed of running a marathon, though he had never run more than one mile. Crushed by initial failures, he went to a coach and asked for direction. The coach gently said to him, "Let's start with a 5K and build from there."

Michael trained with newfound purpose, breaking the
marathon dream into much more manageable mini-goals.
Every small victory amidst every mile run and every drop
of sweat became fuel for his motivation. Over time, his
confidence truly soared. He found himself enjoying the
entire process of setting realistic goals, which transformed
not only his fitness level but also how he perceived
persistence and commitment.

Exercises & Reflective Questions: Dressing Your Course

Exercise: The Goal Map

Take a few minutes to write down a goal you would like to
achieve. Break it down into smaller, workable steps. Make a
timeline for each step and visualize the celebration of each
milestone as it is achieved.

Reflective Questions:

What is one goal that looks impossible but, once broken
down, might actually be a series of small, real steps?

Healing Moment:

Close your eyes and envision what your life may be like
when you reach your goals. Think about how you got
there. What are those smaller steps, those moments of
triumph that helped to secure your success? Permit
yourself to feel the pride and joy inherent in each step you
took.

Episodic Cinematic Perspective: Your Epic Life Story

Imagine yourself as a hero in an ambitious film. The first challenge is an overwhelming ambition, one that is too great to accomplish. However, as the story unfolds, a guide, perhaps in the guise of a friend or a book, enables you to temper your ambition. You begin to view climbing the mountain as a way, step by step, to rejoice in each summit conquered. The camera pulls out, showing a glorious transformation in the trajectory of your journey: not only to achieve your goals but also to better understand yourself.

Discussions of Change: A Podcast Dialogue

Setting Realistic Goals: A Conversation with Sam and Mira

Join Sam and Mira as they delve into the power of setting realistic goals in self-improvement.

Sam: "Mira, sometimes the concept of improvement really feels overwhelming. How do you keep your goals so realistic?"

Mira: "It begins with recognition, Sam. I discovered that overambition can work against me. Getting smaller objectives gives me a sense of momentum."

Sam: "That makes a lot of sense. Can you give me an example of what made this click for you?"

Mira: "Absolutely! I wanted to write a book, but I started with the goal of writing just one page a day. Those pages accumulated pretty quickly, and I actually completed my manuscript much sooner than I ever thought possible."

Sam: "It's pretty incredible how a proper mindset can make what would be a monumental task less daunting. Any advice for listeners?"

Mira: "Remember, every great achievement starts with a step. Focus on what you can do today; it'll pave the way for tomorrow."

As they close their talk, they remind us that no matter how small the step we take, it carries tremendous power.

Power of Realistic Goals: The Message of Motivation

A universal truth emerges: realism in goal-setting is a compass guiding us to our achievements.
Self-improvement by no means requires grand gestures; instead, it requires steady and minor steps taken over time. Acceptable goals are a good way to develop resilience and maintain motivation while at it.

Therapeutic Approach & Healing Moment: Directed Reflection

Healing Moment:

Take a deep breath. Close your eyes and choose one goal that frightens you. What comes to mind? Do they stem from fear or ignorance? Let go of those thoughts lightly and picture a more manageable version of that goal. Change "I will" into "I can start with…. Let this transformation create a glow of lucidity and determination inside you.

Final Thought: The Seeds of Success

The road to self-improvement thrives on achievable goals that motivate and strengthen. Every thought you nourish corresponds to an action you can take. Staying vigilant regarding your aspirations and working toward them over time empowers you with a promising future. Remind yourself that it is through the small seeds of effort that your largest successes grow on their limbs.

Reflective Question/Closing Thoughts:

As you tread upon your road to self-improvement, ask yourself the following questions:

- What strategies do you employ to set realistic goals? Are those goals realistic?
- What can you do today for a better tomorrow?
- How will this mindset of small victories change your journey?

This journey, of course, is yours alone. You feed it with well-defined, realistic goals, a way of tapping into the power to write your own script.

9.3) The Stress of Aspiring Growth and Lived Gratitude

Introduction: Share Your Inner Topography of Growth and Gratitude

Imagine standing at the crossroads of aspiration and appreciation, where each step toward growth is lived in that deep sense of thankfulness. What if today you welcomed the idea that your journey of self-improvement beautifully be linked to a thankful heart? Growth does not mean reaching out for more but instead appreciating and being thankful for what exists within and around you. Every task, whether it's personal, professional, or spiritual in character, seems to mold your reality based on both your desires and your ability to be thankful.

Quotes: Words That Ground Us

- *"The greatest of virtues is gratitude, since it is the parent of all the others." - Cicero*
- *"The roots of all goodness lie in the soil of appreciation for goodness." - Dalai Lama*

- *"Success is not the key to happiness. Happiness is the key to success. If you love what you are doing, you will be successful." - Albert Schweitzer*

These quotes reveal the intricate dance of striving and appreciating. Gentle reminders, they focus true success on the foundation of thankfulness, making our quests for growth not just about reaching new heights but also about cherishing the journey.

Poem: Harmony in Aspirations

"In the garden of your soul, where dreams take seed,

Nurtured by appreciation, that's how we succeed.

As we wander and wonder, every step a delight,

Growth blooms in thankfulness, a wondrous sight.

What you aspire to holds meaning and light,

When paired with thankfulness, your heart takes flight.

Each pursuit you run toward, each achievement you meet,

Tastes sweeter when enjoyed, as you pause to appreciate"

It encapsulates the growing interlink between growth and gratitude. It reflects a desire that can germinate if it is nurtured by appreciation to make realities that are rich with meaning and fulfillment.

Relevant Stories: A Journey of Balance

Let's use the case of Marcus, an entrepreneurial spirit who was so consumed by his zest for success that he never had time to enjoy living. Every day was spent in a headless chase after the next big deal, the next milestone all at the cost of happiness and fulfillment. One evening, after yet another grueling day, a mentor raised his head and reminded him, "Marcus, never forget to celebrate the little triumphs. Gratitude is the foundation for sustainable achievement."

Initially, he resisted the situation, but then he began to see the positives: encouraging team members, loyal customers, and the lessons learned from failure. He realized that a routine practice of gratitude could lead to great changes. His levels of creativity increased, partnerships thrived, and he became satisfied with life. His work in balance between growth and appreciation of what he already had made his ambitions highly fulfilling and an adventure in itself.

Exercises & Reflective Questions: Balance Growth and Gratitude

Exercise: Daily Balance of Growth and Gratitude Journal

Write down one goal you are working toward and one thing you are grateful for in your life each day. Look back at the week and reflect on how the two elements interact. What does this reveal about the harmony between growth and gratitude in your own life?

Reflective Questions:

In all your striving for goals, do you ever stop to look at just how far you've come? What would change if you took time to consider your steps forward?

Healing Moment:

Take a few quiet breaths in a calm space. Consider something you've achieved recently or at least moved closer toward growing into. Now, let gratitude well up for that moment. How can this build upon your pursuit of future goals?

Cinematography Approach: Your Life as the Journey of Harmony

Imagine yourself as the protagonist in a great movie, trying to navigate your way through the choppy waters of ambition and appreciation. In the opening scene, you're in the hustle, racing heart, racing thoughts, always seeking that next accomplishment. The plot thickens with the appearance of that significant mentor who teaches you a very important lesson: growth blooms best in a garden full of gratitude.

As the camera pans out, you see your very own journey of ambition balanced with appreciation. Challenges are met with a new lens, weaving in gratitude into a new daily narrative. The climax reveals you at the precipice of possibility, having achieved what once seemed impossible, your success now so deeply rooted in a season of appreciation for the journey itself.

Conversations of Change Podcast Dialogue

Aspirations and Appreciation: A Conversation between Sarah and Jason

Let's join Sarah and Jason in an interesting conversation about the balance between aspirations and appreciation.

As Jason said to Sarah, "Sarah, in your experience, how does one keep that delicate balance between striving for his objectives and practicing gratitude?"

Sarah: "It's all about perspective, Jason. When I shifted my focus towards what I already had, I realized that my drive for growth didn't decline; rather, it thrived. It was liberating to recognize my current blessings while still reaching for the stars."

Jason: "That's deep. For many, it may feel like growth calls for non stop hustle. How do we change that narrative?"

Sarah: "If we acknowledge the small wins, celebrate our progress, and remind ourselves that every step forward, no matter how small, is a success worth appreciating."

Jason: "That is so true! Beautiful, beautiful circle. The more we appreciate, the more motivated we are. Any final thoughts for our listeners?"

Sarah: "Begin in a small way. Reflect each day on one thing you appreciate and one thing you are working toward. This simple practice can weave mindfulness throughout your journey, creating a rhythm of balance that amplifies both growth and gratitude."

As their conversation ends, listeners are encouraged to embody both ambition and appreciation in their lives, aware that each fuels the other in a meaningful dance of self-discovery.

The Power of Mindset: Embracing Both Sides

At the core of this journey is an undeniable truth: the power to transform your experiences lies in your mindset. As you tread on the thin line between growth and gratitude, acknowledge that they actually complement each other and enrich your life. By working on appreciation, you prepare fertile ground for your ambitions to bud and flourish.

Therapeutic Approach & Healing Moment: A Guided Reflection

Therapeutic Moment:

Breathe in deeply, hold it, and slowly exhale. Think of a time when you felt proud of your accomplishments. Now, reflect on how grateful you felt at that moment. What were you appreciative of along the way? Let this reflection inspire you to recognize how striving and appreciation come together in your life: each promotes the other and expands your potential.

Final Thought: The Intertwined Path of Growth and Gratitude

Every step you take toward growth has the potential to be enriched by the practice of gratitude. The two are intertwined, each illuminating the path in its unique way. As you become aware of the balance you can create, consider how nurturing this relationship opens new avenues for transformation and fulfillment.

Reflection Prompt/Closing Thoughts:

As you continue to navigate your journey, take a moment to reflect:

- How does gratitude enhance your journey toward your aspirations?
- In what ways can you incorporate the practice of appreciation into your daily life?
- What would it feel like to hold both gratitude and ambition as your guiding stars?

You will then understand that achieving a balance between seeking development and gratitude turns your life experiences into larger tapestries of fulfillment and success.

Chapter 10: Integrating the Nine Steps into Daily Life

Introduction:

It is not that balance is something achieved by one big effort but has to be done daily, as you read through how to integrate the nine aspects of life into your mundane life, making them move in tandem. Conscious infusion of these aspects, like health, relationships, or growth, makes a living reflection of the values closest to your heart. By very small, intentional actions you can turn ordinary days and nights into a reflection of your purpose and live enduring fulfillment. The key is to be consistent and mindful, using every moment to build the life you want. Let's start living your balance today.

10.1) Strategies to Integrate the Nine Dimensions into Daily Lives

Introduction: Weaving the Threads of Life

Imagine a tapestry of life where the threads of your daily experiences weave with the nine basic dimensions: health, relationships, career, personal growth, finances, recreation, environment, spirituality, and contribution. What if you could learn to weave these vital strands together harmoniously into your everyday living, as if creating a masterpiece that reflects your values and aspirations? Each moment spent nurturing these focuses not only forms your daily experience but also shapes the larger picture of your life's journey.

Quotes: Wisdom on Integration

- *"Success is not the key to happiness. Happiness is the key to success. If you love what you are doing, you will be successful."* — *Albertitzer*
- *"Life is inherently risky. There is only one big risk you should avoid at all costs, and that is the risk of doing nothing."* — *Denis Waitley*
- *"Your life does not get better by chance; it gets better by change."* — *Jim Rohn*

These quotes indeed encapsulate a strong message: in the integration of different areas of life, one needs to be deliberate and take action. With every bit of attention, you empower not just your life but also that of others.

Poetry: Life Weaving

"In the loom of daily grind,

Threads of purpose intertwine.

Health and happiness, like colors bright,

Weave a tapestry of light.

Tenderness is the thread that sews,

Stitching together every dream it flows.

Careers are aligned upon passion's thread,

Creating pathways where hearts are led."

This poem speaks to the nature of weaving your life together, highlighting the beauty of intentional integration across different realms. It illustrates that every thread contributes to a rich existence, representing an important balancing act between focus and energy.

Relatable Stories: A Shift in Routine

For instance, take Mark. His life seemed disjointed. His job was at full strength; those who knew him would say that he was utterly devoted to his work but his daily life felt sparse in delight. Personal relationships became an afterthought, and so did his health. Then one evening, he chanced upon the concept of the nine areas of focus woven into one's life.

He hesitated at first, not knowing where to begin. Gradually, he changed his habits, starting with private time: a workout in the morning, weekly family dinners, and time for reflection. As he began to incorporate these changes, profound new connections started to emerge. For example, a simple morning run could now ignite his creativity, a weekly family meal restored familial bonds, and focused time for reflection opened doors to growth. Mark experienced an organic shift; indeed, the integration of these dimensions streamlined his life from disorganized chaos to cohesive order.

Exercises & Reflective Questions: Weaving Your Tapestry

Exercise: The Daily Reflection

At the end of each day, take five minutes for reflection. Determine which of the nine areas received the most attention. Were some not addressed at all? Now choose a small intention for the next day based on one of the less attended areas.

Reflective Questions:

Of the nine, which area of focus has felt most rewarding in your life lately? In what ways might you enhance this focus further?

Healing Moment:

Close your eyes and breathe in deeply. Now imagine the nine fields of concentration as rich threads within a tapestry. How do they reflect your life now? And when we weave in new threads of colorful sheets or patterned ones, how will you make them flow smoothly into your daily endeavors?

Cinematic Approach: Life's Montage

Imagine seeing your life as a beautifully edited montage. Moments flash by: a brisk morning walk, laughter over dinner, stillness in meditation, meaningful work projects, acts of service in the community all interwoven through the film of your life.

As you pan through each scene with your camera, you'll feel each of the emotional tones reflected. One shift from chaos to harmony reveals the very different emotional flows you embrace and focus on with intention. Every moment, every choice is like an edit that refines the essence of your life's story, weaving a powerful arc full of joy, balance, and purpose.

Conversations of Change: A Dialogue of Discovery

The Weaving of Focus: A Conversation with Sarah and Tom

Sarah: "Tom, can you believe how easy it is to feel disjointed if we don't weave our focuses together?"

Tom: "Absolutely, Sarah. So many times, I get so immersed in work that I forget about the other areas. How do you balance these out?"

Sarah: "I start my morning with a brief check-in, perhaps journaling about how I can nourish my health, relationships, or growth within daily tasks."

Tom: "That's really cool! If we set time aside for these focuses, it feels more possible."

Sarah: "For sure! It's about making intentional decisions not just seeing how things play out, but creating and even planning."

Tom: "In a sense, it's almost like being proactive instead of reactive."

Sarah: "Yes! Every small shift compounds into something beautiful. Let's remember to embrace these practices together, cultivating a life of intention."

Mindset Power: Focusing Your Focus

The need for harmony is profound in bringing clarity to your journey. Every intention set and every area of focus that you bring into your life has the potential to transform your daily routine into a sanctuary of possibility. The more you incorporate these vital threads into your life, the more aligned you become with your true self.

Therapeutic Approach & Guided Shift: A Smooth Transition

Therapeutic Moment:

Take a deep breath in. Exhale slowly. Imagine standing in front of a loom, threads from your life just waiting for intentional touch. Feel the weight of each area of focus in your mind. Imagine how they can knit together seamlessly. What new routines might you establish that truly weave all nine areas into the fabric of your life?

Final Thoughts: The Tapestry of Your Life

The complexity of your tapestry will be in your hands. Every focus and every intention you set weaves into the overall beauty. As you intertwine these nine areas within your daily lives, you create a life that reflects who you truly are, embracing growth, joy, and fulfillment.

Reflection Prompt/Closing Thoughts

While weaving this tapestry, reflect on the following:

- What areas of focus do you feel most alive and strong in your life today?
- What steps can you take to proactively become more deeply engaged in these areas?
- Imagine that you are living this way namely, with each part of yourself interwoven, alive and vibrant, moving toward all that has meaning.

The artistry of your rhythm holds you. In this tapestry, you have the chance to create a life that resounds with depth, intention, and aliveness.

10.2) Your Custom Action Plan for Balance and Satisfaction Forever

Introduction: Tailoring Your Personal

Imagine you're at a fork in the road as life's turning. You have a map of what you want ahead of you. Now imagine if I told you that achieving balance and satisfaction is not everyone's road. Every path is tailored from the weave of your values, desires, and aspirations. By realizing that life always needs personal stratification, you can now wade through the thicker fibers of life meaningfully, like an artist carefully chiseling out a masterpiece. Then, you will be able to have a life that portrays who you really are and guides you to experiences that favor balance and happiness.

Quotes: Beacons of Guidance

- *"The only limit to our realization of tomorrow will be our doubts of today." — Franklin D. Roosevelt*
- *"Success is not the key to happiness. Happiness is the key to success. If you love what you are doing, you will be successful." — Albert Schweitzer*
- *"Your life does not get better by chance; it gets better by change." — Jim Rohn*

These words deeply reflect on our lives. They remind us that balance is not only wishful thinking but an actual reality born out of our intent and actions.

Poem: The Journey Awaits

"Undefined paths, drawing near with hope,

And dreams. We press ahead. Step by step we make

Choice after choice in quest of more joy.

Our hearts come awake.

A life in balance, dance of grace,

Fulfillment in a loving space.

Weave your path, one breath, one thought,

And every lesson taught along the road."

This poem forms the concept of creating a self-designed action plan that will illuminate the path toward balance and fulfillment. This poem underscores the idea that every movement, however small, counts and weaves into the beautiful tapestry of your life.

Relatable Stories: Finding the Flow

Consider Mark, a dedicated professional who often felt overwhelmed by unending responsibilities. For years, he struggled with prioritizing his needs and desires, believing that sacrificing his own joy was the path to success. One day, after a particularly intense week, Mark encountered an article that posed a remarkable question: "What small step can you take today to nurture your own well-being?"

With renewed interest, Mark replied. He devoted one hour a week to a beloved hobby of painting. Gradually, this small act brought satisfaction that spilled over into other domains of his life. His relationships began to flourish, his creativity soared, and his sense of overall balance dramatically shifted. By developing an individualized action plan, Mark's passion became the genesis of living life as an equilibrium of enjoyment and purpose.

Exercises & Reflective Questions: Mapping Your Journey

Exercise: Your Balance Blueprint

Now, take a minute to think about the areas of your life that need better balance whether it's work, relationships, health, or personal passions. Then, write an action step for each area that aligns with your greater vision for fulfillment. So, if it's healthy, your action step might be to walk a little bit each day or try a new healthy recipe.

Reflective Questions:

What does fulfillment mean to you? What are the first elements that come to your mind when you imagine the epitome of a balanced life?

Healing Moment:

Sit comfortably, breathe deeply, and visualize your dream day. What makes you feel good? How would the environment around you be? Let this vision lead you to your personalized action plan that cultivates the seeds of what you want.

Cinematic Approach: Your Life's Visual Script

Picture your life as a compelling narrative unfolding daily. Each scene is a choice, a thought, an action, a moment of awareness. The protagonist of this story (that's you!) faces challenges but also moments of inspiration. Imagine discovering a mentor who offers valuable guidance: "Life thrives where choices align with purpose."

As you view the scenes, you see how each 'script' you write through your actions ends with a climax of fulfillment. The credits roll at the close, telling the story of a life well-lived, one that speaks to your core.

Dialogues of Change: Dialogues of Growth

Reflecting Your Action Plan: A Chat with Taylor

So, let's get into the conversation with Taylor and dive right into the notion of having an individually tailored personal plan for balance and fulfillment.

Taylor: "Let's talk about how each of us wields the brush to pen our own script. Having a personalized action plan isn't about tasks anymore but about leaning into what resonates with our very essence. Think about every day as presenting a new canvas for us to paint our desires."

Taylor continues: "My friend Ella was overwhelmed by life's demands. One day, she decided to gain clarity on what brings her joy. Simple journaling led Ella to outline what a balanced week looked like, you guessed it: creativity and quiet time each week. It wasn't about adding tasks but about becoming the actual definition of what a fulfilled life would mean for her."

Taylor muses: "If you view your action plan as a living, breathing document, then you make it a powerful tool for growth. So I ask you: How will you walk through the world with intention and awareness?"

Power of Mindset: A Message of Possibility

Within you lies immense potential to redesign your reality. Every thought you entertain forms the backdrop of the life you are going to lead. As you embark on this process of designing a customized action plan, keep in mind that you are the architect of your experiences. By perceiving challenges as opportunities, your path unfolds easily and logically.

Therapeutic Approach & Healing Moment: A Guided Visualization

Therapeutic Moment:

Shut your eyes and breathe in. Recall the most recent test that has shadowed you. What thoughts arose? Were they drenched in fear or wrapped in hope? Gently let go of the limiting mindset, opening up to empowering thought processes. See within you the balance that is right and true. Maybe instead of saying, "I can't," you say, "How can I make this work for me?" Invite this shift inside of you and empower it with possibility.

Final Thought: Creating Your Reality

This is where the journey toward continuous equilibrium and fullness commences. Every intention you bring into the world is a stroke in your own one-of-a-kind masterpiece. As you build this sensitivity around your thoughts and actions, you attune to the life you want to create. Remember, your personal action plan is not just a list, it's a lifestyle, a creation of infinite possibilities.

Reflection Prompt/Closing Thoughts:

In this moment of self-discovery, take a step back to reflect:

- How intentional are you in crafting your action plan?
- What small, meaningful adjustment can you incorporate into your life to enhance your sense of balance?
- What might your daily experience feel like if lived through a lens of fulfillment and purpose?

Your life is a dynamic canvas just waiting to be painted with the colors of your desires and dreams. With every deliberate step, you open pathways into a reality that truly reflects who you are.

10.3) Reflective Exercises to Evaluate and Rewrite Life Priorities

Introduction: Realign Your Compass

Life is an appropriate moment to assess your life priorities, those guiding stars that orient you across the vast ocean of existence. Do you ever reflect on whether those priorities truly represent your deepest values and goals? Imagine what your life could become if you chose to rethink what matters most. Every thought that springs to mind concerning your priorities can alter your course. Are you drifting, or are you driving purposefully to a place that speaks to who you are?

Quotes: Food for Thought

- *"An unexamined life is not worth living." —Socrates*
- *"Your priorities are like the stars in the sky; they guide you but might be obscured by the clouds of distraction." —Anonymous*
- *"The secret of your future is hidden in your daily routine." —Mike Murdock*

These words remind us of the importance of introspection in life. They emphasize that it is a quest to determine what is important for ourselves.

Poem: The Essence of Priorities

'The river flows; it carves its way,

Through rock and time, come what may.

So too, you must choose your path,

In light, in joy, in aftermath.

Prune the branches, cut away the weeds,

What matters most? Plant those seeds.

With every choice, a flower blooms,

Reflect and see what truly looms."

This piece embodies the essence of nurturing priorities. Just as the seasons change in nature, we also need to fertilize whatever in life represents something precious to us. Good intentions through thoughtful prioritization tend to sow growth and abundance.

Stories From Life: Shift of Focus

Think of Alex, the young professional lost in the chaos of life's demands. Chasing deadlines and accolades, he was filled with conviction that success was the sole route in life. But deep down, something felt missing: his true passions lay forgotten. After coming clean to a sage friend, she pushed him to reevaluate his priorities. It was with hesitant curiosity that Alex took the first step of reflection. He wondered what would happen if he aligned his work with his love for the arts. Soon, he began making tiny changes workshops, expressing creativity. He found that his life was more vibrant, and opportunities that once felt too far from him started shining on his horizon. With renewed priorities, Alex transformed his world by aligning daily actions with his innermost passions.

Exercises & Reflective Questions: Clarity Cultivation

Exercise: The Priority Inventory

Devote time every week for the next month. Create a list of what you currently consider to be your highest priorities: relationships, career, health, personal growth, and so on. Rate each one from 1 to 10 based on how satisfied you feel in that area. Reflect: Am I spending my time on what is most important?

Reflective Question:

Where are you feeling energized about life? Where in your life is it draining you? What could you do to shift some time and energy to create more positive differences?

Healing Moment:

Close your eyes and breathe. Imagine an average day in your life. Which activities elicit joy and fulfillment? Now, imagine a day constructed around your most important priorities, with all your passions and purposes infused into it. How will you make this a reality?

Cinematic Approach: Your Life as a Story

Imagine life as one epic film. You're center stage, under pressure from competing priorities. The script unfolds, or rather stumbles along with you amidst all the clutter of distractions. And now, your mentor, a figure, a book, a moment of clarity appears, teaching you the power of intentionality. Critical moments illuminate your path: bold choices spring forth as you reach a climactic scene, embracing your true priorities. The crowd cheers at the strength it takes to clean out one's life and listen only for what really matters.

Dialogues of Change: Lessons Learned from Conversation

Reflections on Priorities: A Conversation with Mia

Mia: "Let us discuss today how we must evaluate our priorities. It is amazing how day-to-day decisions shape our experiences but often lead us astray. We end up so engrossed in the minor details that we lose sight of the big picture.

"I remember a friend, Julie. She was always hectic but unhappy. One day, she read a journal prompt that asked her to dream about life as she would want it to be. In envisioning her ideal life, she discovered that too much hustle took from her the desire to form relationships. It made her yearn for connections more than for hustling herself into productivity.

"It's fascinating, isn't it? Introspection can illuminate what's been veiled by the routine of our lives. By becoming creators of our own narratives, we can ensure that our choices reflect who we truly are and what we genuinely want."

The Power of Evaluation: A Motivational Note

Every minute spent contemplating and changing your priorities attests to your commitment to living a fulfilling life. As each change serves as a ripple that shapes both your experiences and those of the people around you, new pathways reveal the world to your potential for discovery.

Therapeutic Approach & Healing Moment: A Guided Experience

Therapeutic Moment:

Take a deep breath. Imagine the landscape of your mind as a trail of a multitude of priorities. Now choose a trail that weighs heavy upon you; a decision that no longer serves you, and simply imagine yourself moving away from it with grace and stepping into more light, meaningful paths. What do you feel in embracing a change like this? Remember that the act of deciding to realign in that process is profoundly self-caring and clarifying.

Final Thought: Journey to Self

Savor the fluidity of change with your priorities because they reflect and respond to your changing self. Every thoughtful choice you make about how you spend your time is an act of self-love that leads you into a life imbued with authenticity and purpose. Your priorities are never set in stone; they're a colorful tapestry of the best of who you have been and who you'd like to become.

Reflection Prompt/Closing Thoughts:

As you embark on this reflective journey, take a minute to consider:

- What are your three latest priorities?
- How closely are they aligned with your values and aspirations?
- What small changes can you make today to bring what you're focusing on and the things you're truly prioritizing more in line?

You can transform your reality through intentional reflection, welcoming fulfillment and purpose into every nook and cranny of your life. Clarity in prioritizing is the first step to crafting a life that reflects your desires.

Thank You!

Thank you for reading ***"The Balance Within: Nine Steps to a Purposeful Life"***. I hope this book has inspired you, grown you, and brought you closer to your authentic self.

Thank you for your support; wishing you balance, healing, and a purposeful journey ahead.

With gratitude,
Shivang Patil